Making More Flower Children

Sybille Adolphi

Making More
Flower Children

Floris Books

Translated by Anna Cardwell

Photographs by Wolpert & Strehle, Stuttgart

Illustrations by Kafitz & Diehl; Böttcher & Bayer, Stuttgart

First published in German as *Neue Blumenkinder für den Jahreszeitentisch*
by Verlag Freies Geistesleben in 2002
First published in English in 2009 by Floris Books, Edinburgh

British Library CIP data available

ISBN 978-086315-685-4

Printed in Singapore

Contents

For Has, Benjamin and Nelia

Introduction

In my first book, *Making Flower Children*, I explained how to put together a seasonal tableau, or seasonal table, and the important role it can play in family life. Made from natural materials like moss and stones, and decorated with hand-crafted flower children, the seasonal tableau is an image of nature; it encourages children to observe and understand the rhythms of nature and offers support and stability in an ever faster-moving world.

Three years on, and the seasonal table has lost none of its appeal for our children. Gradually mystery is giving way to curiosity. What are these flowers? Where do they grow? What kind of parts do they have? Do they smell? Which animals visit them? Are they poisonous or not? The children still like listening to stories about flowers and nature and often make up their own little tales, inspired by the seasonal table.

This interest in and understanding of nature is very important for children. It encourages them to be aware of nature, to learn to respect plants and animals, and to realise that they too have a responsibility towards looking after their environment.

Out of this understanding, children develop a desire to make their own flower children. Naturally, the instructions given for adults are too difficult for children to follow. So I have included a short chapter which shows how seven-year-olds and upwards can make their own simple flower children.

As children make flower children, you will realise that they have different standards than we adult perfectionists. Let them use their creativity, even if it does not match your own ideas. These meadows of flower children have their own special beauty: the beauty of your children. By making their own flower children, the seasonal table becomes more interesting for children as they have been allowed to contribute towards it.

The first chapter in this book repeats the basic instructions given in my first book, *Making Flower Children*, and so contains all the information needed, as well as plenty of new ideas.

Basic Patterns

The following pages describe the basic patterns for making the different flower children.

The patterns are meant as a guideline for beginners. Once you have mastered the basic forms you will be able to make up your own flower children. All you need are good observational skills in nature and some imagination.

Making the head

It is most important to achieve a smooth head without folds.

Take your time making your first heads. After you have made a few you will have mastered the seemingly difficult processes and they can be made without much effort.

The body size varies from flower child to flower child, and it is mentioned in the instructions for each flower child.

MATERIALS
Wool yarn
Unspun sheep's wool
Thin knitted cotton, 2 3/4 in (7 cm) long, sewn
    into a tube, width depending on head size
Skin-coloured cotton knit, square, 2 3/8 in (6 cm)
    long
Tying off thread

It is important to use soft, stretchy cotton knit for the head. Thick cotton knit will always leave some folds.

The following are the instructions for making a head for a large flower child.

1. Wind a solid ball out of wool yarn remnants, about 3 in (8 cm) in circumference.

2. Gather the cotton knit tube close to the edge at the top end. To do this, sew the thread (always use a double thread) in at the one side and gather round to the other side. Pull the thread tight and sew it in well. Now turn the tube right way out.

3. Place two layers of not too thick unspun sheep's wool in a cross on top of each other, place your yarn ball in the middle of the cross and fold up the ends of the cross (see figure on page 10). Tie up the head right below the yarn ball with strong cotton thread.

4. Put the knitted cotton tube over the wool head, pull it down tightly and tie it right below the yarn ball. To obtain a really round head, roll the head firmly back and forth a few times. Grasp the wool hanging out of the head firmly with one hand, pulling at the cotton knit. If there is now a gap between neck and head, tie up the head again nearer the wool ball, untying the old thread first.

5. Now tie the eye and chin line to form the head. Use a strong, unbreakable thread as it needs to be pulled very tightly. Linen thread or book binding thread are good for this.

For tying up use a knot that is easy to pull tight, but does not come undone by itself.

Beginners can wind the knot over their hand and then slip the loop over the doll's head. To make the knot, lay the thread around the back of your hand. Wind one end around your hand

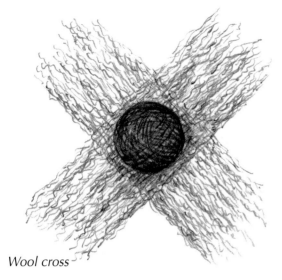

Wool cross

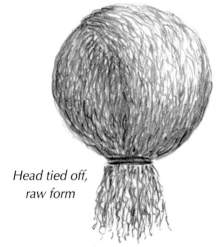

Head tied off, raw form

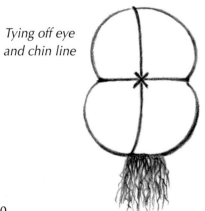

Tying off eye and chin line

again. Both ends will now be lying along your palm. Put your thumb over one end to hold it tight. The other end is threaded behind your thumb and from below through the lower thread. This end is drawn up again from below through the lower and then the upper thread (see opposite).

Pull on both ends. If you can feel constant pressure around your hand the knot is done correctly. Take the loop off your hand and put around the middle of the doll's head. Pull the knot to make the exact eye line. If it does not work at first, you can easily loosen the knot again by pulling the ends back and forth. If the thread keeps slipping you can fix it at the right height by sticking two pins into the head at the eye line until you have pulled the thread tight. Take out the pins again afterwards. Make sure the eye thread is in the middle of the head. Choose the best side of the head for the face. Pull the thread tight again, tie another knot and push the knot to the ear point. Sew in the threads by passing them right through the head with a long needle, then cut off the ends.

Make the same knot over your hand for the chin line. Lay it vertically over the head, pull it tight and knot it once. Sew a cross over the meeting point of the eye and chin threads at the ear with the thread, then pass the thread through the head and cut off the ends (see figure to left).

6. Now you can form the back of the head. Because the threads have been sewn together at the ear points, the eye line cannot slip anymore and you can pull the thread of the eye line down at the back to the neck. Use a crochet hook for this. Push it under the thread from above and pull the thread down with it to the neck thread.

7. Take your square piece of cotton knit (make sure the rib runs vertically over the head) and lay it over the face to test the face. If the eye line appears too deep, lay a small piece of unspun wool over the thread. You can adjust the depth to your taste. If you cannot see an eye line at all through the cotton knit, then you need to re-tie it.

If you want to make a small nose (e.g. for gnomes), then sew a few stitches right under the eye line below each other, or even on top of each other. Keep checking what it will look like by stretching the cotton knit over the face.

If you are happy with the face, then stretch the cotton knit over it. The upper edges should not overlap over the top of the head, but the fabric should overlap at the back. Push all the folds at the neck to the back and tie up the head under the chin again. Sew up the back seam making sure the cotton knit is stretched back. To finish, sew up the 'fontanel' on the top of the head.

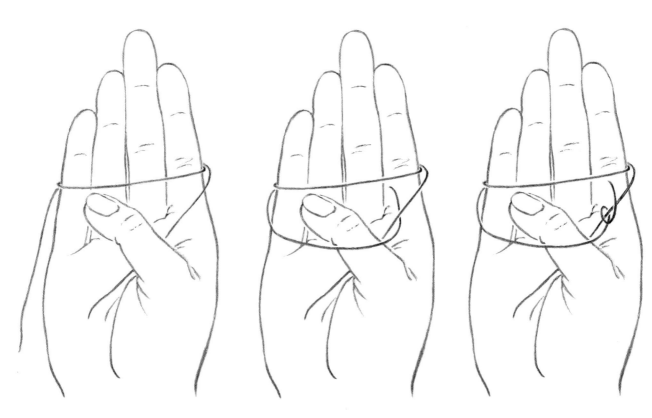

Making a knot for tying up

Making the dress for a flower girl with long skirt

MATERIALS

Craft felt 4 5/8 in x 5 3/4 in (12 cm x 14.5 cm)
for the skirt

Craft felt 2 3/8 in x 4 5/8 in (6 cm x 12 cm) for
the top

Tips

You do not need to leave a seam allowance for these patterns. Always sew with a double thread. The dress is made out of two pieces, a top with sleeves and a simple skirt as a lower part. The shape of the sleeve depends on the petal of the respective flower children, so it varies from flower child to flower child.

Start with the lower part. Lay the larger square piece of felt down in front of you and fold the longer half up as shown above. This will leave a thin single edge, making it easier to sew the top onto later. Always double the felt for stability. Now fold the felt again lengthways and sew it together with a narrow seam. Sew in the thread, but do not cut off the end. Use the thread to sew a gathering seam around the thin single edge. Let the remaining thread and needle hang down and turn the garment the right way round.

Now sew up the top after cutting the pattern out of the smaller piece of felt. Sew up the sleeve seams and fold the garment in half to cut the neck opening. Do not cut the neck too big. Turn the garment right way out.

Take the head, cut off all the threads hanging down and tease out some of the sheep's wool. Twist this wool tightly together and carefully push it through the top neck opening. The felt will stretch a bit. Pull the top into shape and push the skirt against it from below. Pull the gathering thread tight and sew the thread in at the back (the seam should always be at the centre of the back).

Sew the top and lower part together with mattress stitch so that the seam is invisible.

If the neck opening is too wide, run a gathering thread around it.

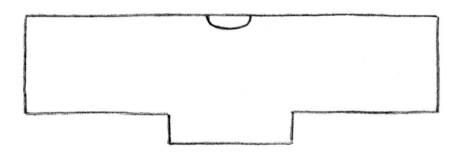

Basic pattern: top, actual size

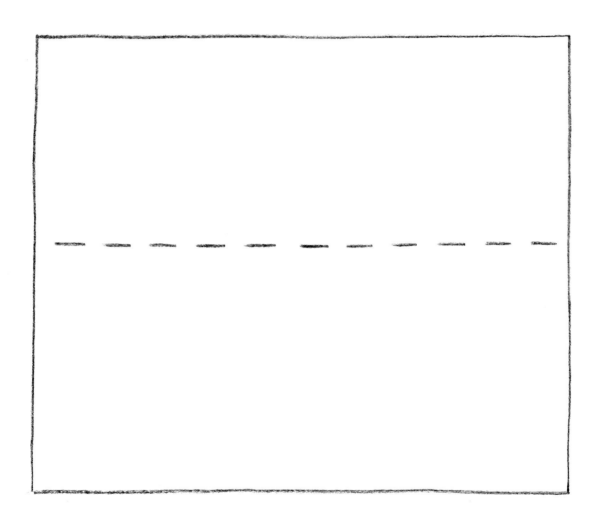

Basic pattern: skirt, actual size

Flower girl with legs

Make the head and body following the instructions for the *Flower boy* (see page 15; head circumference 2 3/4 in (7 cm), arm length 3 1/2–3 7/8 in (9–10 cm), leg length to fit the sewn cotton knit leg).

Wind light-coloured, unspun sheep's wool thinly and evenly around the arms and legs.

Legs

Sew the cotton knit legs according to the pattern. Copy the pattern onto the cotton knit (make sure the rib is running vertically) and cut it out. Fold over the legs lengthways so that the legs are on top of each other. Pin them together and sew with backstitch from the top to the start of the legs. Fold the cotton knit back so you can see two legs again, the cotton knit is double. Sew up along the inside of the leg, sewing a curve at the groin. Turn the right way round and stretch well with a ball-point pen or similar object.

Adjust your pipe-cleaner leg which has been wound with unspun sheep's wool (see page 15) to the length of your cotton knit legs. Bend the feet over about 1/8 in (5 mm) so the sharp pipe-cleaner cannot pierce through the cotton knit. Then pull the cotton knit legs over the pipe-cleaners.

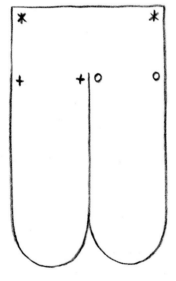

Cotton knit legs, actual size

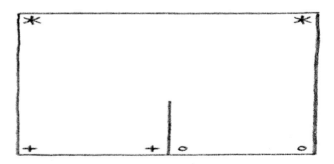

Underpants, actual size

Underpants

Make the underpants out of felt, cotton or silk. Vary the length depending on the flower child and personal preference. Sew the back seam with blanket stitch, then the leg seam. Turn the underpants the right way out and put them on the doll. Depending on pattern and preference, sew a running seam around the base of the underpants' leg.

You can also make the underpants out of a piece of elastic lace. Sew the piece together at the back (measure around the stomach first). Make the legs by sewing the piece together at the groin with a few stitches.

Put the underpants on the doll. Stuff a piece of fluffed unspun sheep's wool into the back to form a bottom. Run a gathering thread around the top of the underpants, pull it tight and sew in the ends of the thread.

Feet

Bend the feet up right angled about 1 in (2.5 cm) with pliers the same as for the flower boy.

Dress

Cut the top of the dress out of felt, cotton or similar fabric. The ends of the sleeves depend on the petals of the flower, and are described in the different flower children patterns.

Sew up the sleeves and side seams of the top.

Make the skirt out of silk, felt or cotton fabric. Make sure the silk has a selvedge to save you hemming it. Cut the skirt out of the fabric according to the instructions for the individual flower children. Run a gathering thread along the top of the skirt and pull it together until it fits the stomach opening of the top. Sew in the threads well and shut the back seam.

Put the top onto to the doll, gather at the neck if necessary, and fasten the hands onto the end of the arms, which should have some unspun sheep's wool wrapped around them.

See if the skirt length is correct and if necessary shorten it. Now sew the skirt to the top with mattress stitch.

Flower boy with legs

Head

Make a head as described above, 2 3/4 in (7 cm) circumference. Shorten the neck to about 1/2 in (1.5 cm). Cut this part right and left (under the ears) until shortly before the tying up the neck thread. Now separate the neck into a front and a back half. These are folded apart.

Body

The body is made out of a frame of pipe-cleaners, over which the clothes are placed.

Take three pipe-cleaners, one for the arms and two for the legs. Bend the leg pipe-cleaners over in the middle and hang them over the arm pipe-cleaner. Twist each leg tightly 2–3 times. Now place the separate neck parts over them and sew first under the arms and then crosswise over the shoulders. Bend the arm pipe-cleaners back to a length of about 3 1/2–3 7/8 in (9–10 cm). The arms should reach just above the head.

Now sew the trousers and put them on. The patterns for the trousers can be found under the instructions for specific flower children. Fold the trousers over so that both legs are on top of each other and sew the back seam to the start of the legs. Sew in the thread and fold the garment so that the seam is in the middle of the back, you will have two legs in front of you. Sew up the inside of the legs. Turn the trousers the right way round and carefully push a ball-point pen or similar object into the legs to make them evenly round.

Only now decide how much to shorten the legs. Take the trousers off again and shorten the legs to the desired length. Do not forget to leave about 1 in (2.5 cm) extra for the foot. Wrap light, unspun sheep's wool around the legs and put the trousers back on. Stuff a piece of fluffy unspun sheep's wool into the back of the trousers to form a bottom. Gather around the top.

Now sew the smock. The patterns can be found in the instructions for the specific flower children.

Sew up the sleeves and side seams. Then turn it right way round and put it on from below. If necessary gather around the neck.

Bend the feet up at right angles about 1 in (2.5 cm) with pliers.

The feet can wear either slippers or boots. Bend them back about 1/8 in (5 mm) at the end to prevent the sharp point of the pipe-cleaner from piercing the slippers or boots.

Shoes

Slippers

Cut the soles out, double and glue the two bits together firmly. Sew the top piece on immediately with blanket stitch, as the glue makes the fabric stiff after it has dried. Round out the front and top evenly with a ball-point pen. Fill the front of the slipper with glue and stick it to the foot. If the felt is very difficult to glue then it is artificial felt and might need a few extra stitches to hold everything in place.

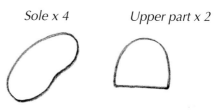

Sole x 4 *Upper part x 2*

Boots

Wrap some more unspun sheep's wool around the feet. Cut out the soles four times and glue them together as described for the slippers. Now you will need a piece of felt 3 in (8 cm) long and as wide as the boots should be high. Sew the piece starting at the back around the sole with blanket stitch. Cut off any extra felt. Try the boot on and shorten it if necessary. Then sew up the back seam and put it back over the foot. To obtain the form of a boot, fold the excess felt at the front into two folds and sew them up to look like laced boots. Tie a bow at the top.

Sandals

Only make sandals for dolls with legs covered with cotton knit.

Cut the soles out double and glue them together firmly. Sew a band of leather or felt over the foot to the right and left of the sole to make the strap.

Important: Different flower children may have different sized shoes. Because of this, always measure the soles against your doll's foot. The sole of the slipper should stick out a bit at the back of the heel.

Arms

Use a pipe-cleaner for the arms. Buy them from a tobacco shop, as they are stronger than craft pipe-cleaners.

Bend the pipe-cleaner back at the end so that the sharp tip cannot poke through the cotton knit. Push it through the arm opening at the back.

Wind unspun sheep's wool around the bent back end for the hands. Be careful to wrap tightly and without twisting the piece of wool. If the wool tears, just lay the end back down and continue winding. The sheep's wool will stick to itself again.

If you find this method difficult, you can make the winding process easier. Unbend the end of the hand, and wind unspun sheep's wool thinly around it just before and just after the bend. Bend the hand back and wind another piece of unspun sheep's wool thinly around the whole hand. The advantage of this is that the wool will not slip over the bend even if it is not wound tightly enough.

Both hands are made out of a folded piece of cotton knit (see figure, remember fabric grain).

Sew them first and then cut them out. Use a thread colour suited to the cotton knit as one can always see the stitches a bit. Make the hands slightly wider at the base, it makes them easier to turn them the right way round later. Then turn them the right way round, using a ball-point pen or similar object to widen them. Take one of the finished hands, pull it over the wound pipe-cleaner hands and fasten it tightly to the arm at about the elbow by winding the thread around it a few times.

Now pull this arm to its right length. For 'children' the arm should only reach to just above the top of the head. Sew a running thread around the sleeve above the 'petals,' pull it tight around the arm and sew it onto the hand.

Bend the other side of the pipe-cleaner so that it is the same length as the first arm and complete it in the same way. The finished arm length should be about 4 $\frac{5}{8}$ in (12 cm).

Fill the skirt from below with some unspun sheep's wool to finish.

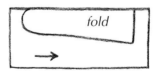

Different hair styles

For the hair styles you can use:
Unspun sheep's wool, long or short staple
Pieces of fur or wool fur fabric
Wool (mohair or bouclé)

Sheep's wool

LONG HAIR WITH FRINGE

To make long hair with a fringe, lay a small strand of wool on the head towards the front. Sew it on with a few stitches. This length of hair is the fringe. For the rest of the hair lay a strand of wool from left to right wide enough to cover the whole head and sew it on with small stitches. If stitches are visible, rub the needle back and forth over the hair so that they disappear under the wool.

You can make braided hair styles out of this long hair, for example plaits or 'monkey swings.'

If you prefer a centre parting for your flower child, lay a small piece of cloth under the centre of the strand of hair wool and sew a straight seam with a sewing machine. Then fasten the strand of hair to the head with a few stitches.

For a shorter hair style use short staple magic wool (unspun sheep's wool), shape it and sew it onto the head with a few stitches. You can usually still make short 'rat tails' or a 'bun' with the ends.

Wig stitched with mohair or bouclé wool

Stitch a cross into the head, and fill in the gaps with further stitches, always guiding the wool under the wool cross. Stitch the fringe slightly irregularly. Then you can carefully brush the hair for a fluffier finish.

Fur or wool fur fabric wig

Tip: Cut wool fur fabric along the cloth under the hair with a sharp pair of scissors to avoid a straight hair line.

Sew the separate triangles together and then put the wig onto the doll. If the wig is too big, correct it at the back. Sew the wig to the head with a few stitches. All the wigs can be made more beautiful by adding a plait or flower head band.

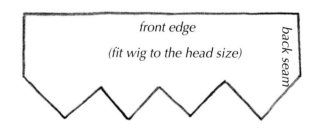

front edge

(fit wig to the head size)

back seam

Making the face

Before you start decorating the doll with a collar, silk dress and petals you can give the doll a personal touch. Although each doll is different despite using the same patterns and clothes, you give it a personal expression when making the face. Because of this, you need to take plenty of time making it. Often your own or your children's faces can be recognised in these faces.

Eyes and mouth

First stick three pins into the face for eyes (two blue pins) and mouth (one red pin). The eyes should always be placed on the eye line and should form an equilateral triangle with the mouth. Careful: eyes that are too close together can appear unfriendly, a mouth that is too high can be mistaken for a nose.

Once you have found the right position you can embroider or draw the eyes and mouth.

EMBROIDERED EYES AND MOUTH

Stitch a suitably coloured double thread from the back of the head, starting with the eyes.

Sew the mouth with a double thread too.

DRAWN EYES AND MOUTH

Carefully pull out the pins and draw small dots in their place with a sharp suitably coloured pencil. Make these dots darker and bigger by pressing the pencil against the cloth until you have the desired size.

You can form the mouth by drawing a line outwards either side of the dot. The line should be straight, not curved up or down. You can make the colour stronger by wetting the pencil.

UNDERLINING THE EYE SOCKETS

Push a needle with a double thread and anchor it firmly under the hair, from the back through the head to the right eye, and push it back into the head $1/32$ in (1 mm) further along. Now pull it tight so that it forms a hollow where the eye should be. Repeat for the other eye. You can now either embroider or draw over the eye socket.

Cheeks

Colour a small piece of cotton knit with red and a bit of brown (coloured pencils are good for this) and carefully pat the cheeks with it. Do not worry if the colour has turned out too strong, it will fade after a short time.

Ways to stitch the eyes

Ways to stitch the mouth

Flower stalks

Make the stalks of the flowers that the flower children are holding out of florist's wire or pipe-cleaners wound with green felt. Pipe-cleaners should be 'shaved' evenly with a pair of scissors.

If the flower has a branched stalk (e.g. a forget-me-not) use thin craft wire.

For better stability always double the wire and twist it firmly together. Leave a small wire loop at the top for some flowers (e.g. a snowdrop) on which to hang the dangling blossom.

Wind green doubled sewing thread around very thin stalks. To do this, spread glue around the bottom of the stalk, stick the thread on to it and wind it tightly upwards, gluing the thread to the top of the stalk again. Do not cut the remaining thread off as you can use it to sew the flower onto the stalk.

Thicker stalks can be wound with felt or florist's tape. Florist's tape is only available in a few shades of green, make sure the felt for the leaves is roughly the same colour, otherwise use felt for the stalk.

Florist's tape sticks by itself so it is not necessary to use glue. Lay the tape diagonally along the bottom of the wire and wind it tightly up to the top of the stalk. Press down slight irregularities.

If you want to use felt, cut a long, $1/16$ in (2–3 mm) thin strip of felt. Check the grain of the felt, in one direction it rips very easily. Put glue onto the bottom of the wire and wind diagonally up the stalk, again gluing the felt to the stalk at the top. Tie as tightly and evenly as possible. It is important to use craft glue for all gluing purposes, because it dries clear and cannot be seen afterwards.

Different stitches used

GATHERING STITCH

Gathering or tacking stitch is used for gathering cloth together, as the name suggests. To make a gathering seam push the needle alternately through a piece of cloth and over a piece of cloth.

BACK STITCH

Back stitch is used for sewing two pieces of cloth together without the cloth gathering if the thread is pulled.

To make a back stitch, pick up a few threads of the cloths to be sewn together, then sew a back stitch that exactly meets the end of the last stitch.

BLANKET STITCH

To make a blanket stitch, push the needle from the back to the front and pull the thread through, leaving a small loop. Push the needle through this loop and pull the thread tight.

MATTRESS STITCH

Use mattress stitch for invisible seams. Lay the two cloths beside each other with folded edges together. Push the needle through one cloth from below; now take a small piece of the other cloth and pull tight.

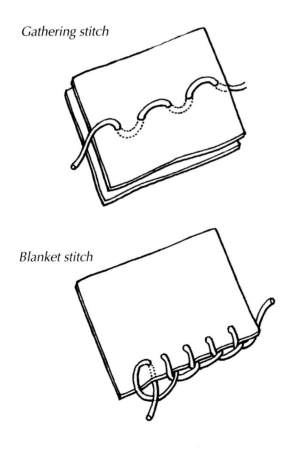

Gathering stitch

Blanket stitch

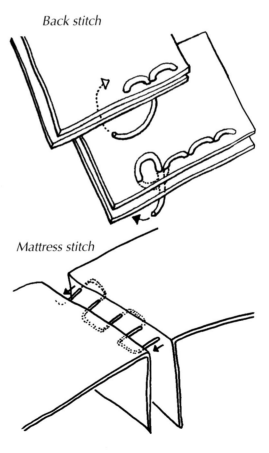

Back stitch

Mattress stitch

Flower children for children

These flower children can be made by children aged seven years and upwards. Depending on their level of skill, they may need help with some of the steps.

The flower children are all made following a basic pattern. They differ solely in colour, shape and decoration.

MATERIALS

Unspun sheep's wool, 6 in (15 cm) long strand
Unspun sheep's wool for the hair
Skin-coloured cotton-knit square 2 1/2 x 2 1/2 in (6 x 6 cm)
Felt for the body
Fabric and felt for decorating

Head

You will need a strand of wool approximately 6 in (15 cm) long. Make a knot in the centre and pull tight. Smooth one of the strands of wool hanging out the knot over and around the knot to make the head. Wind a strong thread around the wool just below the knot; this is the neck. The head should be approximately 3 1/8 in (8 cm) in circumference. Young or inexperienced children can leave the head like this, without features (see purple flower child).

For the next step, cut a 2 1/2 x 2 1/2 in (6 x 6 cm) square out of cotton knit and lay it over the front of the face with the rib running vertically. The top edge should be level with the top of the head. Pull the knitted fabric together tightly at the back, bind it off at the neck and sew the back and top shut.

Use unspun sheep's wool for the hair. Sew it to the head with a long needle, pushing it in from left to right and from front to back.

Body

Cut a piece of felt, 3 1/2 x 4 in (9 x 10 cm). Fold it in half, but not exactly in the centre — leave a thin border for running the gathering thread through. Sew the back seam. Turn right side out and run a gathering thread around the top. Push the head into the top and pull the gathering thread tight. Sew in the thread ends.

For smaller flower children, halve the pattern.

Decoration

You can make capes and other garments out of fabric. Use felt for making leaves or calyxes, if desired. If you want, sew a flower or hat to the head.

Spring

The long winter is finally coming to an end and beneath the earth nature gradually awakens. Tiny green shoots push up out of the ground and fat buds are waiting to burst into flower once the sunbeams warm up the air. The first spring flowers herald nature's awakening. In the early mornings, birds greet the new day with joyful song.

A small cheeky boy, the Root child, looks around inquisitively. Everywhere he gazes there are new things to see. He quietly observes the flower elf helping the first flower children to dress themselves in their new clothes. She is telling them what happens to the earth in spring. She tells them about the sun that will warm them, of the moon and the stars at night, the rain that waters them and of the wind that quietly rocks them and carries their seeds away. Each flower child listens attentively in anticipation of what awaits them. Only the Root child wonders: "If there is so much to see and learn here alone, then think how much more there is in the whole world. I want to travel through the seasons and find out which I like best." So off he sets on a journey through the seasons.

Root child

MATERIALS
See basic pattern for *Flower boy with legs*
Green velour for the trousers
Brown felt for the slippers and hat
Brown fabric for the shirt
Light brown fake fur for the hair
White silk for the bundle

Small stick for the bundle
Stuffing wool
Brown fabric paint

Make the body according to the instructions for *Flower boy with legs*, head circumference 3 in (8 cm). Make a small nose (see page 10).

The finished arm length is 4 in (10 cm) plus 3/8 in (1 cm) extra per hand to fold back. The finished leg length is 2 in (5 cm) plus 3/8 in (1 cm) extra per foot to fold back.

Cut the trousers out of green velour and sew them together as shown. If necessary, run a gathering thread around the waist.

Cut out the smock and sew the sleeve seams using blanket stitch. Run a gathering thread around the neck and wrists and pull tight when the smock is on the doll.

Cut the hat out and sew it together with small blanket stitches (see diagram page 21). Glue the

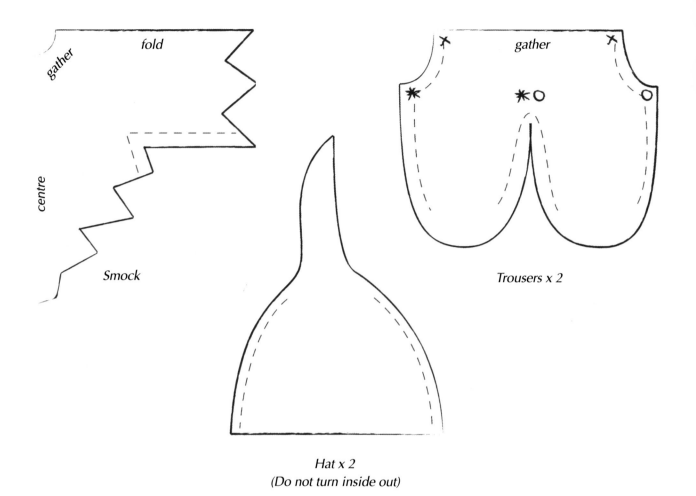

gather

fold

centre

Smock

gather

Trousers x 2

Hat x 2
(Do not turn inside out)

hat to the hair. Twist the tip of the hat firmly between your fingers to make it root-like.

Make felt slippers for the feet (see page 16).

Use a small sewing needle or pin to make the freckles. Carefully dip the tip into brown fabric paint and dot over the nose.

Cut a square piece of silk for the bundle, put stuffing wool in the centre and knot the ends crosswise over a small stick.

Forsythia child

Flower child

MATERIALS
For body and dress, see basic pattern for *Flower
girl with long skirt*
Yellow felt for the dress
1 pipe cleaner
Unspun sheep's wool for the hair

Make the body according to the instructions for
Flower girl with long skirt, head circumference 3
in (8 cm). Use the pattern for the sleeve edge.

Flower

MATERIALS
1 pipe cleaner
Craft wire 5 x 5 1/2 in (14 cm) lengths
Brown strip of felt approximately 3/16 in (0.5 cm)
  wide
Yellow felt for the flower
Green felt for the leaves
Yellow and green sewing thread
Transparent craft glue

Closely crop the hair of the pipe cleaners.

Bend one of the pieces of craft wire in half and
twist lightly to make a flower stalk. Leave a small
loop at the top. Do the same with the other 4
lengths of wire.

Now attach the flower stalks to the pipe
cleaner: firmly twist the craft wires at different
places around the pipe cleaner so they stick out
by approximately 1 in (2.5 cm).

Apply a small dot of craft glue to the base of
the pipe cleaner. Glue one of the brown strips of
felt to it and wind it around the stalk until the first

flower stalk branches off. Add another drop of
glue and wind the felt up to the wire loop. Glue
tight. Continue in the same way until all the stalks
are covered in brown felt.

Thread a double thickness of yellow sewing silk.
Wind it around the topmost loop until the loop is
entirely covered with yellow thread. Sew 7 loops
using the same thread to make the stamens.

Cut the flowers out of yellow felt following the
pattern shown. Push one of the flowers over the
stalk. To do this, cut a small cross into its centre.

Fold the petals upwards and wind yellow sewing silk tightly around the base to securely fasten the flower to the stalk.

Spread some glue around the calyx and press it tight. This allows you to model it a little.

After you have made 2–3 flowers, push a leaf up the stalk from below; cut a small cross into its centre first. Fold the leaves up and wind green sewing silk around the base.

Continue as described above with the remaining flowers and leaves.

To finish, cut open the loops (stamens) and shorten them to the desired length.

Twist the petals lightly between forefinger and thumb to give them their distinctive shape.

Then bend the flower stalks into shape.

Flower

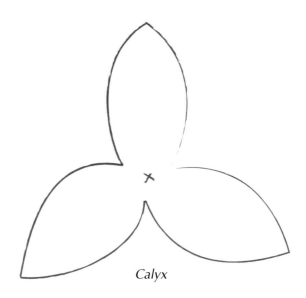

Calyx

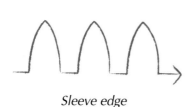

Sleeve edge

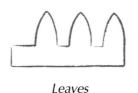

Leaves

Elf

MATERIALS
Cotton-knit tube
Skin-coloured cotton knit
Unspun sheep's wool
Pipe cleaner
Strong thread
White velour for the shirt
White silk and white tulle
Small piece of coloured sheep's wool

Make a head, circumference 2 1/2 in (6 cm) (see basic patterns). Cut slits into the fabric that is hanging below, to the right and left below the ears, almost up to the tying-off thread.

Cut the shirt out of white velour and sew the sleeves and sides. Then turn it right side out and cut the neck opening.

Take the head, separate the sheep's wool and the fabric hanging down below lengthways and push a pipe cleaner through the gap. Place the wool and fabric back over the pipe cleaner and wind a piece of strong thread around everything to hold it all in place.

Make the arms 4 in (10 cm) long. To make the hands, wind a thin strand of sheep's wool around the ends of the pipe cleaners (be careful not to twist the strand of wool). Then bend back the ends of the pipe cleaners and wind a thin layer of sheep's wool around this double part. This gives the hands a nice shape. Cut two circles out of cotton knit and pull them firmly over the hands. Bind off with a strong thread, making sure there are no folds.

Put the shirt on and run a gathering thread around the neck, pull tight and sew the ends in well.

Cut the dress out of white silk. Sew the sides up until 3/4 in (2 cm) before the fold and turn right side out. Cut the neck opening and pull the dress over the doll's head.

Push the sleeves up to the shoulders, fold the edges back to make a small hem and sew tight with a few stitches.

Cut the cloak out of silk and fasten it to the right and left at the wrists, and tothe back at the centre of the neck with a few stitches.

Cut the wings out of tulle and fasten them to the back with a few stitches.

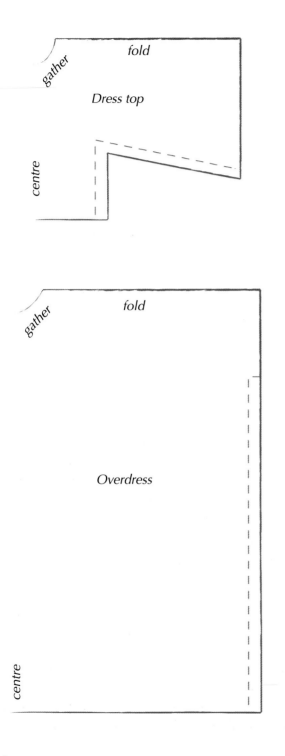

gather

fold

Dress top

centre

gather

fold

Overdress

centre

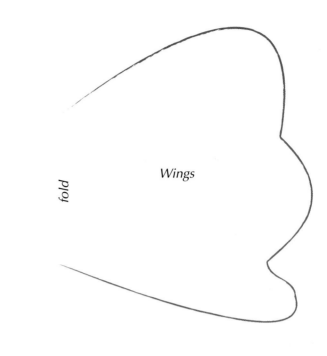

fold

Wings

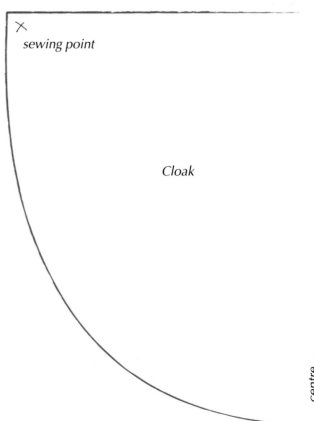

✕

sewing point

Cloak

centre

Anemone child

Flower child

MATERIALS
See basic pattern for *Flower girl with legs*
White felt for shirt and collar
White silk for the overdress
Elastic lace for the underpants

Make the flower child according to the instructions for *Flower girl with legs*, head circumference 2 3/4 in (7 cm).

Cut the shirt out of white felt. Sew the seams, turn right side out and put it on the flower girl.

Cut a 4 3/4 x 2 3/4 in (12 x 7 cm) square out of the white silk, if possible keeping the selvedge at the bottom. Sew the back seam. Fold the dress with the back seam in the centre and cut out arm holes. Run a gathering thread around the neck and put the dress on the doll.

Cut the collar out of white felt, run a gathering thread around the neckline and put it on over the dress.

Flower

MATERIALS
Craft wire, 12 in (30 cm) long
Green felt for the leaves
White felt for the flower
Green and yellow sewing silk
1 green glass bead
Florist's tape
Purple coloured pencil
Transparent craft glue

Fold the craft wire in half and push the glass bead into the centre. Knot 8 threads of green sewing

silk around the wire. Push the knots right up to the bead and spread the threads around it evenly. Together with the bead this makes the flower receptacle. Knot approximately 20 threads of yellow sewing silk under the knots of the green sewing silk to make the stamens. Spread them around the stalk evenly. Cut open all the loops and shorten them to approximately 1/16 in (2 mm).

Cut two sets of petals out of white felt. Cut a small cross into the centre and push them up the stalk. Offset the petals and glue them to the stalk.

Wind green sewing silk firmly around the knots and about 2/16 in (3 mm) of the stalk.

Cut three leaves out of green felt. Glue a 1 1/4 in (3 cm) long piece of craft wire to the stalk of each leaf, pushing the stalk around the wire (see diagram). Wind florist's tape around the wire just below the leaf for about 3/4 in (1 cm). Using the wire not covered by florist's tape, attach all three leaves approximately 1 1/4 in (3 cm) below the flower to the stalk. Now wind florist's tape around the rest of the stalk.

Colour the base of the petals with a purple pencil. This is easier to do if you wet the pencil slightly beforehand.

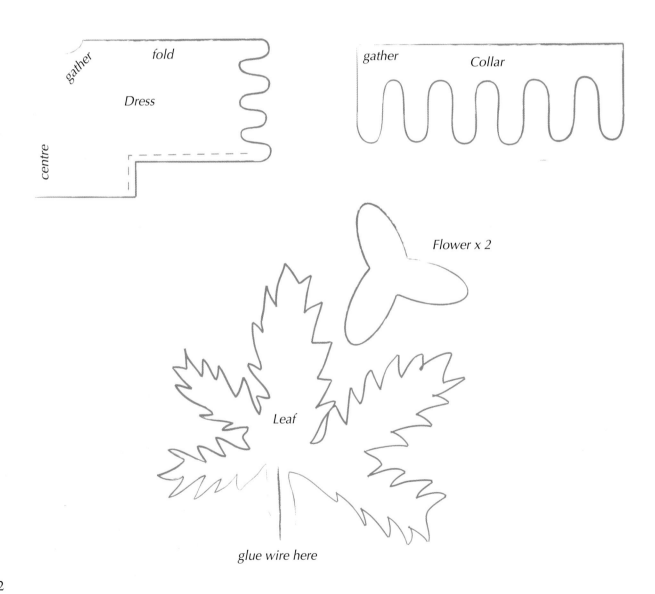

Crocus child

Flower child

MATERIALS
Basic shape and dress see *Flower girl with legs*
Yellow felt for the dress
Unspun sheep's wool for the hair

Make the flower child according to the instructions for *Flower girl with legs*, head circumference 2 3/4 in (7 cm).

Cut the dress out of yellow felt, sew the side seams and put it on the flower child. Run a gathering thread around the neck and wrists and pull tight. Starting at the back of the dress under the right arm, run a gathering thread to the left arm to slightly gather the dress in at the back.

Crocus flower

MATERIALS
Craft wire, 12 1/2 in (32 cm) long
Florist's tape
Yellow and green felt
2 small yellow glass beads
A small length of yellow embroidery silk
Yellow sewing thread
White coloured pencil
Transparent craft glue

Bend the craft wire in half and twist the ends together. Flatten the loop at the top with a pair of pliers. The craft wire is the stalk for both flowers.

Glue a glass bead to each end of the wire as a pistil. Leave them to dry well.

Take a double thickness length of sewing thread, glue one end below one of the beads and wind approximately 1 1/4 in (3 cm) down around

the wire. Glue the other end tight. Do the same for the other bead.

Cut two 1 1/2 in (4 cm) long pieces of embroidery silk, and knot them to the wound wire, approximately 3/8 in (1 cm) under the bead. Untwist the ends of the embroidery silk with a needle to make the crocus stamens.

Now cut two sets of the inner and outer flower out of felt. Make the base of the outer petals slightly wider than the inner petals (see diagram) so that you can glue one over the other. Glue the base of the inner petals around the wire, leaving the pistil sticking out of the flower about 1/4 in (7 mm). Glue the open side together so that all the petals are the same distance from each other. To make the petals curve inwards, spread some glue over the inside of the petals and bend them inwards. Let the glue dry well. Offset the outer petals between the inner petals and glue them tight. Bend the outer petals inwards too, as described above.

The second, slightly more closed flower is made in a similar way to the one described above, but glue the single inner petals together at the edges, then offset the outer petals again and glue them tight to the inner petals.

Wind florist's tape around the rest of the craft wire. Bend the stalk, not exactly in half, to make one longer and one shorter flower. Then cut the stalk at the bend.

Cut the leaves out of green felt and draw a white leaf vein in the centre with a white pencil. Wet the tip of the pencil to make the veins more visible. Now glue the leaves to the base of the stalk.

Place a flower into each arm of the flower child.

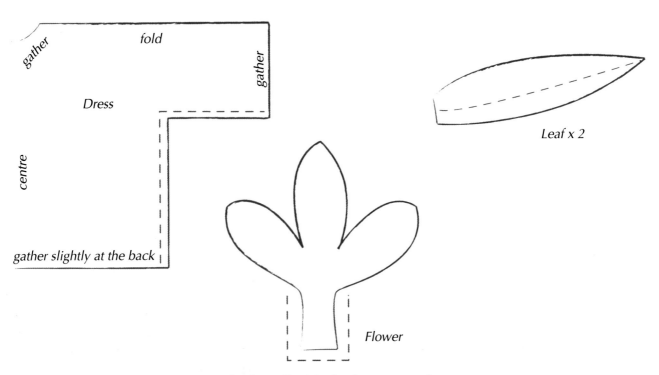

make the stalk wider for the outer petals

Apple-blossom child

Flower child

MATERIALS

For basic shape and dress see
Flower girl with legs
Skin-coloured cotton knit
White felt for the dress
Green felt for the jacket
Yellow magic wool for the hair
Elastic lace for the underpants

Make the flower child according to the instructions for *Flower girl with legs*, head circumference 2 in (5 cm), arm length 3 in (8 cm), leg length 1 1/8 in (3 cm).

Cut the shirt and skirt out of white felt and colour the fabric lightly (see instructions for Flower). Sew the shirt seams and put it on the flower child. Run a gathering thread around the neck and pull tight. Sew the back seam of the skirt and gather at the waist. Put the skirt on the flower child; the shirt should hang over it. Now pull the gathering thread tight and sew in the ends.

Cut the jacket out of green felt and sew it tight under the arms with two or three stitches.

Use the instructions below for making the flower for the hat (make it without the stamen). Glue the flower hat to the hair of the flower child.

Flower

MATERIALS

Pipe cleaner, approximately 1 1/2 in (3.5 cm) long
Green felt for the calyx and stalk
White felt for the flower

Yellow sewing thread
Transparent craft glue
Red coloured pencil

Wind a thin strip of green felt around the pipe cleaner from top to bottom to make the stalk. Using yellow thread, sew about 20 loops to the top end for the stamens. Glue the five white petals around these loops to the stalk. Cut the calyx out of green felt. Cut a small cross into the centre and push it up the stalk from the bottom. Glue it to the stalk and petals. Cut open the loops of the stamens and shorten them to the length desired. Rub the wet tip of a red pencil against a piece of cotton knit. Carefully rub this piece of cotton knit over the outside of the white felt petals to colour them slightly.

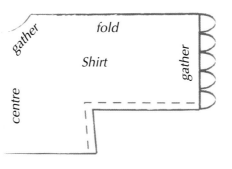

gather *fold*

Shirt

gather

centre

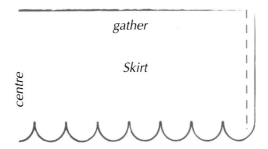

gather

Skirt

centre

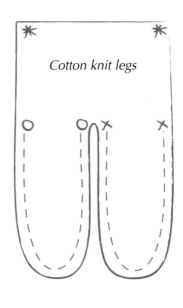

Cotton knit legs

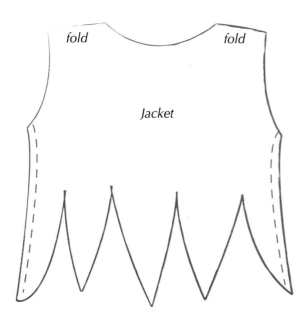

fold *fold*

Jacket

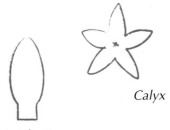

Petal x 5

Calyx

36

Ladybird

MATERIALS
Material for a head, circumference 2 1/2 in (6 cm)
Red felt for the wings
Black velour for the body and cap
Black felt for the feelers
Black pipe cleaners
Black sheep's wool for the hair
Transparent craft glue

Make a head, circumference 2 1/2 in (6 cm). Make a small nose for the ladybird (see basic patterns, page 10).

Cut the body out of black velour, sew the seams shut and turn right side out. Push the head into the body. Run a gathering thread around the opening, pull tight and sew the body to the head with a few stitches.

Glue a few bits of black sheep's wool to the head for hair.

Cut the cap out of velour and sew it together at the back. Put it on the head and sew to the body with mattress stitch.

Now cut the feelers out of black felt and sew them to the cap.

Cut the wings out of red felt, glue black dots to them and sew a black seam along the centre of the wings. Run a gathering thread around the top of the wings, pull slightly and sew the wings to the body with a few stitches.

Bend the pipe cleaner back to make the legs 2 1/2 in (6 cm long). Fasten the legs to the centre of the stomach with a few stitches.

Embroider a mouth and eyes.

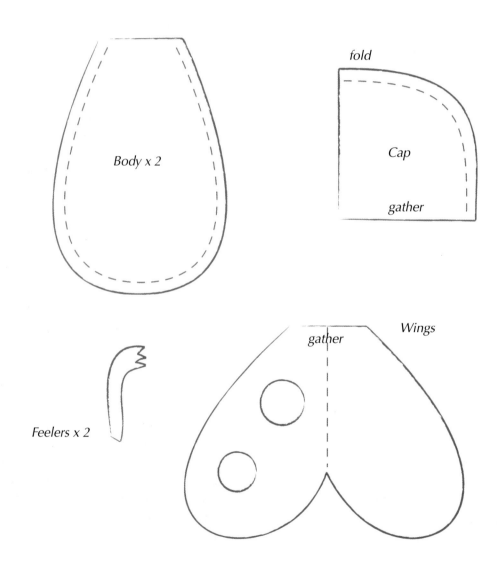

Body x 2

fold

Cap

gather

Feelers x 2

gather

Wings

Violet Child

Flower child

MATERIALS

For the basic shape and dress, see
  Flower girl with long skirt
Dark purple felt for the jacket
Light purple felt for the apron
Yellow magic wool for the hair

Make the flower child according to the instructions for *Flower girl with long skirt*. This flower child is slightly smaller, so use the pattern given here for the skirt and jacket, using dark purple felt. Head circumference is 2 3/4 in (7 cm). Cut the apron out of the light purple felt, sew the side seams together and put it on the flower child. Run a gathering thread around the body under the arms, pull tight and sew the ends in.

Flower

MATERIALS
Craft wire
Green felt for leaves and calyxes
Dark purple felt for the flower
Light yellow strand of wool
Yellow coloured pencil
Florist's tape
Transparent craft glue

Cut two sets of the flower pattern out of dark purple felt. Cut 5 pieces of craft wire, each 1 1/2 in (4 cm) long and glue them to each petal, starting at the base (see diagram). Glue the second flower over the first one to cover the wires. Glue the base of the petals firmly around the wires, approximately 3/8 in (1 cm) upwards.

You will need an 8 in (20 cm) long piece of craft wire for the stalk; bend it in half and wind florist's tape around it. Glue yellow wool to the upper end of the stalk for the pistil. Place the stalk over the base of the flower so that the pistil will remain visible. Sew the flower around the stalk until the petals are 5/8 in (1.5 cm) apart.

Glue the calyx from below to the flower and stalk.

Cut out the (second) leaf and glue a 2 ½ in (6 cm) long piece of craft wire wound with florist's tape to the centre of the leaf. Wind florist's tape approximately ³/₈ in (1 cm) around the lower end of leaf stalk and stalk.

Colour the upper two petals just beside the pistil with a yellow coloured pencil.

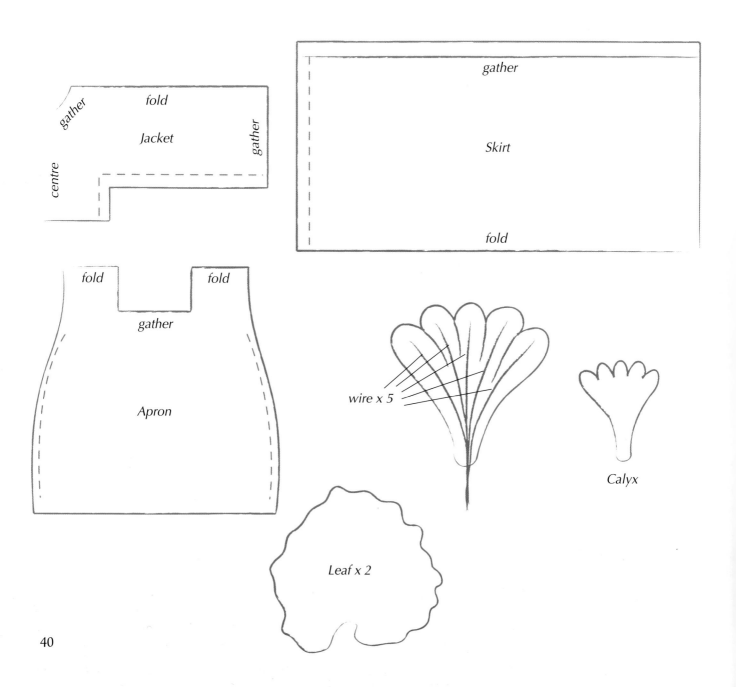

Primrose child

Flower child

MATERIALS

For basic shape see *Flower girl with legs*
Yellow silk for the dress
Green felt for the jacket
Elastic lace for the underpants
Yellow strand of magic wool for the hair

Make a flower child according to the instructions for *Flower girl with legs*. The head circumference is 2 3/4 in (7 cm). See the pattern and instructions for Cornflower child for the dress (page 53).

Cut the jacket out of green felt, sew it together under the arms with a few stitches and put it on the flower child.

Sew the underpants out of elastic lace, following the instructions on page 15.

Flower

MATERIALS

Craft wire 5 x 4 1/2 in (11cm) lengths
Yellow silk for the flower
Unspun sheep's wool
Green felt for the calyxes and stalks
5 yellow glass beads
Transparent craft glue

Cut five sets of the flower out of yellow silk. Glue a yellow glass bead to the tip of each of the craft wire lengths. Glue the bottom part of each flower, below each bead, to the stalk. Wind some unspun sheep's wool around the base of each flower to make it slightly thicker.

Cut five sets of calyxes out of green felt and glue them around the thickened flower bases. Wind a thin strip of green felt around the craft wire approximately 3/4 (2 cm) below the calyx. Wind a green strip of felt around all the wires down to the base of the stalk.

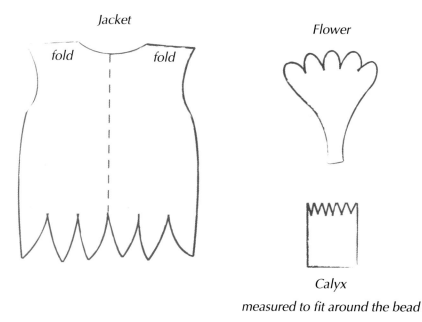

Jacket

fold   *fold*

Flower

Calyx

measured to fit around the bead

Cuckoo-flower child

Flower Child

MATERIALS

For basic pattern, see *Flower girl with legs*
Purple silk for the dress
Elastic lace for the underpants
Yellow magic wool for hair

Make the flower child according to the instructions for *Flower girl with legs*. Head circumference is 2 3/4 in (7 cm).

Cut the dress out of purple silk. Only cut the arm edging once the dress has been put on. Run a gathering thread around neck and wrists, approximately 3/16 in (0.5 cm) away from the edge. Sew the underpants out of lace as described on page 15.

Flower

MATERIALS

Craft wire 8 x 1 1/2 in (4 cm) lengths; 1 x 8 in (20 cm) length
Purple silk for the flower
Yellow and green sewing silk
Florist's tape
Transparent craft glue

Cut five sets of the flower out of purple silk. To make the pistil, wind yellow sewing silk three to four times around the wire, approximately 3/4 in (2 cm) below the end of the wire; knot and glue it tight. Sew 12 small loops with yellow sewing silk around the pistil for the filaments. Only cut them open once the flower is completely finished. Push the flower from below almost right up to the end of the craft wire and glue it tight. The pistil should stick out approximately 1/8 in (3 mm). Wind green, double thickness sewing silk around the rest of the wire. Wind it closely, particularly over the yellow sewing silk. Repeat these instructions for the remaining 4 craft wires.

To make the closed flowers, glue a very small piece of purple silk around the top half of the wire and press down well. Wind green sewing silk around the stems of these flowers too. The silk of the closed flower should stick out approximately 3/16 in (0.5 cm) above the stalk. Make two more closed flowers.

Take the 8 in (20 cm) long piece of wire for the main stalk and fold it in half. Twist both ends together lightly and wind florist's tape around the stalk. Wind the 8 flower wires around the top third of the main stalk and wind green sewing silk around them all. Make sure the sewing silk is the same colour as the florist's tape.

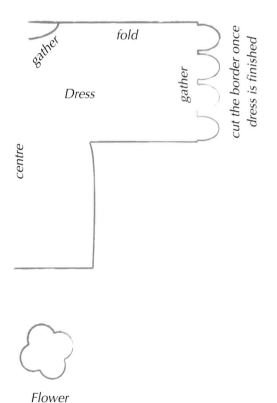

Flower

Buttercup child

Flower child

MATERIALS
For basic pattern, see *Flower girl with legs*
Yellow velour for the dress
Elastic lace for the underpants
Yellow magic wool for the hair

Make the flower child according to the instructions for *Flower girl with legs*. The head circumference is 2 1/2 in (6 cm). Use the pattern provided for the dress and the pattern given for the apple-blossom child for the legs (see page 36).

Cut the dress out of yellow velour; sew it together and turn right side out. Run a gathering thread around the neck.

Sew the underpants out of elastic lace as described in the basic patterns (see page 15).

Flower

MATERIALS
Craft wire
Wooden beads 2 x 1/16 in (2 mm); 1 x 3/16 in (5 mm)
Yellow felt for the flowers
Green felt for leaves and calyxes
Yellow sewing silk
Florist's tape
Transparent craft glue

Take a 9 1/2 in (24 cm) long piece of wire for the stalk, fold it in half and twist the ends together lightly. Push a wooden bead 1/16 in (2 mm) onto one ends; wind florist's tape around the stalk and the bead. You will need to press the florist's tape down well around the bead. Sew many small loops over it for the filaments with yellow sewing silk. Only cut them open once the flower is finished.

Cut 5 petals out of yellow felt and glue them to the stalk around the bead. Cut the calyxes out of green felt and arrange them evenly below, gluing them tightly.

Take a 3 in (8 cm) long piece of wire for the second flower; bend it in half and proceed as described above.

For the closed flower, take the large bead $3/16$ in (5 mm) and push it onto the tip of a 1 $1/2$ in (4 cm) long piece of craft wire bent in half. Wind florist's tape around both the wire and the bead. Press the florist's tape well around the bead.

Gather the three stems together at the top third of the long stalk and firmly wind florist's tape around them all. Attach the leaves where the stalks meet by winding green sewing silk around them tightly.

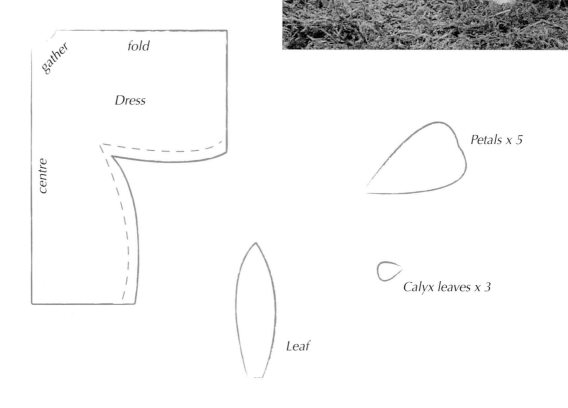

gather   *fold*

centre

Dress

Petals x 5

Calyx leaves x 3

Leaf

Summer

The little Root child notices the weather is getting even warmer. The strong sun sends burning rays down to the earth and many animals and flowers look for a shady spot to take shelter during the day. When the ground is dry and hot, dark clouds in the sky are a welcome sight as they promise the relief of rain.

During the long summer days the Root child likes to sit by the rippling brook. With his feet dangling into the cool, clear water, he listens to the buzzing of the bees. Colourful butterflies flutter around playfully in the meadow and crickets hop merrily.

The Root child lies back and watches thick white clouds pass by overhead. He often laughs out loud at the funny shapes they make. "I like it here," he thinks. "But there must be more to learn. Who knows what else there is to discover…" And so the Root child continues his journey of the seasons.

Chicory child

Flower child

MATERIALS
For the basic shape, see *Flower girl with legs*
White silk for the dress
Light blue felt for the skirt

Make a body according to the instructions for the *Flower girl with legs*. Use the pattern provided for the sleeve edging. Head circumference is 2 3/4 in (7 cm).

Make the dress top according to the instructions given for the Flower girl with long skirt. Dress the doll and run a gathering thread around neck and sleeves, pull tight.

Cut a light blue strip of felt, 1 3/8 x 4 1/4 in (3.5 x 11 cm), for the skirt, cutting tiny zigzags into the bottom edge. Sew the back seam. Sew in the thread, but do not cut it off, use it for running a gathering thread around the waist. Once the skirt is made, pull the gathering thread until the skirt fits well. Make sure the back seam is at the centre of the back. Sew the skirt to the top with a few stitches.

Make blue sandals for the feet.

Flower and stalk

MATERIALS

Light blue felt for the flower and border
Green felt for the calyx
Pipe cleaner, 6 3/4 in (17 cm) long
Florist's tape or green felt
Florist's and craft wire
Bean-shaped small beads
Light blue small glass bugle beads
Transparent craft glue

Using light blue felt, cut the flower border with 14 flowers as shown in the pattern.

Push a bean-shaped bead over the tip of a 1 3/4 in (4.5 cm) length of florist's wire and wind florist's tape or green felt around it and the stalk. Leave a small length of wire sticking out above the bead for the glass bugle bead. Press the florist's tape around the bead well.

Cut the calyx out of green felt and glue it around the top third of the bead. Bend the leaves right apart at the top.

Run a gathering thread around the edge of the flower border and pull tight until the centre gap disappears. Sew the flower to the florist's tape and the felt of the calyx. Make sure the calyx leaves are still visible.

Now push a glass bugle bead over the tip of the wire and glue tight. Attach a further 5 bugle beads to the centre of the blue flower by threading them up one after the other and sewing them tight.

Wind florist's tape around the pipe cleaner, which is the main stalk. Then wind tape around the 3 florist's wire stalks, each 3/4 in (2 cm) long when finished, to attach them and their flowers to the stalk. Push a bean-shaped bead over the tip of each side stalks and wind florist's tape around

them and the bead. Push a bead over the tip of the main stalk and wind florist's tape around it too. Now cut calyxes for each bead and glue them to the top third of the beads.

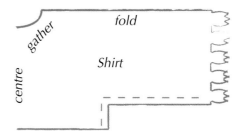

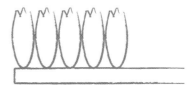

Flower border with 14 petals

Calyx

Globe flower child

Flower Child

MATERIALS
For basic pattern, see *Flower girl with long skirt*
Yellow felt for the dress
Yellow magic wool for the hair

Make the flower child according to the instructions for *Flower child with long skirt*. Head circumference is 3 in (8 cm).

Cut the dress with petal border out of yellow felt. First run a gathering thread around the top of the longer dress, pull it tight and sew the thread in well. Place the shorter dress piece over it. Run a gathering thread around the top, pull it tight and sew the thread ends in well.

Flower

MATERIALS
Craft wire
2 pipe cleaners
Green and white felt
Yellow silk paint
Florist's tape or green felt
Transparent craft glue

Cut two sets of the three corollas out of white felt (six flowers). Cut a small cross into the centre of each corolla for pushing the stalk through later. Take one of the smallest corollas, cover half of each petal in craft glue and glue the petals together. Put craft glue around the top of the corolla and press inwards to give the flower a spherical shape. Push the second smallest corolla over the first, offset the petals and glue tight, letting the petals overlap. Glue the two larger

corollas to the outside of the previous ones. To finish, press one of the two largest corollas around the petals below so that the whole flower looks like a globe, offset the petals and glue tight. Glue the last flower from the base again. Pull the petals over the blade of a pair of scissors to make them bend inwards. Make the second flower in the same way.

Wind florist's tape or thin strips of felt around each pipe cleaner. Lay the pipe cleaners together and attach them at the centre by winding florist's tape around them both.

Now cut the calyxes out of green felt, cut a small cross into each centre and push them onto the two stalks. Put craft glue over the tips of the stalks. Push the flowers over the tips of the stalks and glue the calyx to them from below.

Glue the leaves to the meeting point of the pipe cleaners. Bend the pipe cleaners a little.

Once everything has dried well, drip silk paint over the flower. This colours them intensely and the flower petals shut due to the moisture. Let the flower dry well. If necessary, repeat this process two to three times. This also makes the flowers smaller and denser.

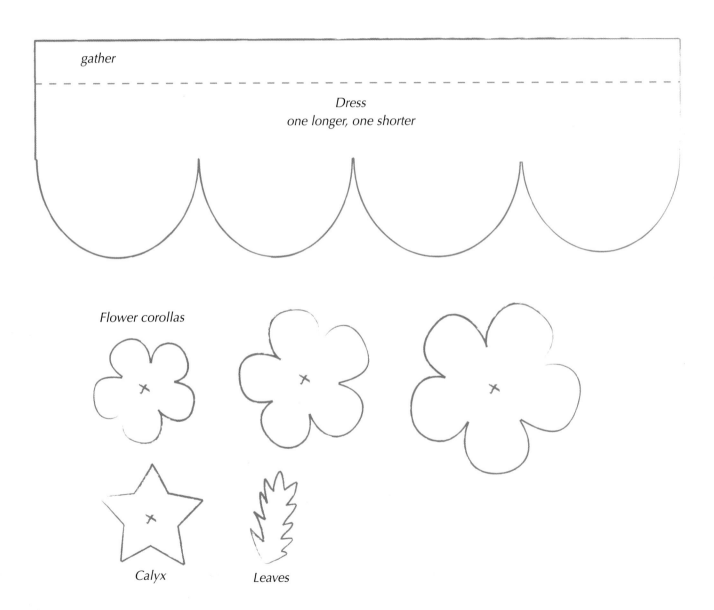

gather

Dress
one longer, one shorter

Flower corollas

Calyx   *Leaves*

Redcurrant boy

Flower boy

MATERIALS
See basic pattern for *Flower boy with legs*
Red felt for the suit
Green felt for the leaves
Brown felt for the hat
Blond fake fur for the hair

Make the body according to the instructions for *Flower boy with legs*, head circumference 2 3/4 in (7 cm).

Cut the suit out of red felt, using the Chicory child pattern (see page 47). Sew it together and put it on the flower boy.

Cut four currant leaves out of green felt, embroider the leaf veins as shown in the diagram and sew to the suit around the neck opening.

Make green slippers for the feet.

Cut the hat pieces out of brown felt. Sew the two upper parts together, turn right side out and sew to the brim with small stitches.

Redcurrants

MATERIALS
Craft wire 1 x 2 in (5 cm) length; 6 x 1 1/4 in (3 cm) lengths
Green sewing thread
Red transparent beads
Transparent craft glue

Wind a double thickness sewing thread around the longer piece of craft wire. Glue the top and the bottom end of the thread tight. Bend the short craft wires in half and wind them around the main stalk so that they stick out by about 3/8 in (1 cm) to the right and left. Glue the red beads (the redcurrants) to some of these short wires. Leave a short distance between the beads and the main stalk. Using a pair of pliers, bend a small hook into each empty length of wire.

Leave the currents to dry well, then cut the surplus wire sticking out of the beads until only a small tip remains.

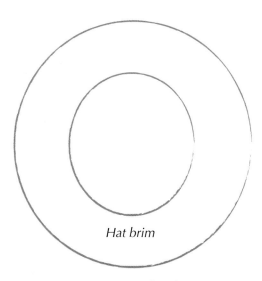

Hat brim

pay attention to head size

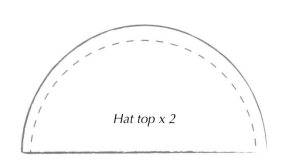

Hat top x 2

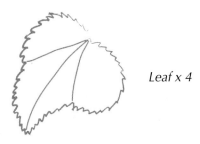

Leaf x 4

Cornflower child

Flower child

MATERIALS
See basic pattern for *Flower girl with legs*
Blue silk for the dress
Green felt for the jacket
Black sewing thread
Elastic lace for the underpants
Unspun sheep's wool for the hair

Make the body according to the instruction for the *Flower girl with legs*. The head is 2 3/4 in (7 cm) circumference.

Cut the top of the dress and the skirt out of blue silk. Cut the sleeve edging once the dress has been put on the flower child (see diagram). Sew the seams of the dress top, run a gathering thread around the neck and put it on the doll. Run a gathering thread around the sleeves, approximately 5/16 in (7 mm) from the edge. Pull the threads tight and sew in the ends. Now cut the sleeve edgings.

Cut a 3 x 5 1/2 in (8 x 14 cm) rectangle out of blue silk for the skirt and fold it in half widthways 1 1/2 x 5 1/2 in (4 x 14 cm). Run a gathering thread along the top (folded) edge, put it on the doll and pull it together a little. Sew the skirt to the top with small stitches.

Make the jacket out of green felt. Cut the front open and embroider front and back using black thread as shown in the diagram. Sew together below the arms with a few stitches and put it on the flower child.

Make the underpants as described in the basic patterns (see page 15).

Once dried (approximately 1 hour), iron the fabric briefly. Cut out two sets of the flower (once each for the open and closed flowers) and snip a small cross into each centre.

You will need an 8 1/2 in (22 cm) long piece of craft wire for the stalk. Bend the wire in half, twist together lightly and wind florist's tape around it. Wind black sheep's wool tightly around the stalk where the calyx will go for approximately 3/8 in (1 cm). Push the flower from below almost up to the tip of the stalk and glue tight. Press the petals upwards slightly. Once the glue has dried, sew lots of loops, approximately 3/8 in (1 cm) long, to the end of the stalk using blue and black sewing silk to make the stamens. Cut them open later.

Make the calyx out of green felt, fit it to the flower, embroider as shown in the diagram and glue to the top of the stalk where the black sheep's wool has been wound.

To make the closed flower, bend a 4 in (10 cm) long piece of craft wire in half, twist together lightly and wind florist's tape around it. Glue the flower tightly to the top of the stalk, without

sewing stamens, and press upwards. Wind black sheep's wool around this stalk too. Cut out the calyx, embroider it as shown, fit and glue it to the lower third of the flower.

Place the end of the closed flower's stalk halfway down the open flower's stalk and wind florist's tape around them both for approximately 3/4 in (2 cm).

To finish, cut out the leaf and glue it to the stalk.

Shamrock child

Flower child

MATERIALS
For basic pattern, see *Flower girl with long skirt*
Two different shades of green felt
6 green transparent glass beads
Red magic wool
Small bast basket

Make the flower child according to the instructions for the *Flower girl with long skirt*, head circumference 3 in (8 cm). Make the dress out of the lighter green felt.

Cut the jacket out of the darker green felt, put it on the doll and sew three beads to each side at the front.

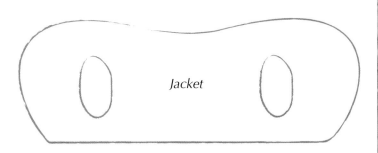

Jacket

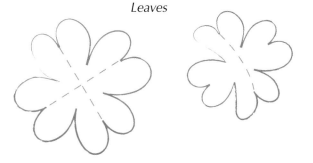

Leaves

Hang the small basket over one of the shamrock child's arm.

Shamrock

MATERIALS
Craft wire
Green felt for the leaves
Florist's tape
Green sewing silk

Cut the shamrock leaves out of green felt and embroider them as shown in the diagram.

To make the stalk, wind florist's tape around a length of craft wire, approximately 1 $1/2$–2 in (4–5 cm). Sew the stalk to the centre at the back of the shamrock leaf with a few stitches.

Poppy child

Flower child

MATERIALS
For the basic shape, see *Flower child with long skirt*
Red felt for the petticoat
Red silk for the overdress
Black glass beads
Thin nylon thread
Black unspun sheep's wool for the hair

Make the flower child according to the instructions for the *Flower girl with long skirt*. The head circumference is 3 in (8 cm).

Cut the overdress out of red silk and sew the back seam. Fold back the fabric approximately $3/16$ in (0.5 cm) around the neck and run a gathering thread around it. This saves you hemming the edge. Put the dress on the flower child and fold the sleeves inwards. They usually stay put without you having to sew the hem in place.

String the black glass beads up to make a short necklace using the nylon thread and tie it around the overdress as a belt.

Poppy flower

MATERIALS
Green pipe cleaner
Red silk for the flower
Unspun black sheep's wool
1 dried poppy pod with stalk
Green felt for the leaf, pod and calyx
Florist's tape
Unspun sheep's wool

Cut 5 poppy petals out of red silk (if necessary starch them first, see Cornflower child, page 53)

and glue them around the poppy pod, offsetting the petals. Glue small bits of black sheep's wool to the top of the poppy pod.

Cut the calyx out of green felt, cut a small cross into the centre and push it up the stalk to the flower. Glue it in place. Wind florist's tape around the stalk.

To make the closed flower, wind florist's tape around a pipe cleaner 1 $1/2$ in (4 cm) long. Cut the pod out of green felt, sew it together, turn it right side out and stuff it lightly with unspun sheep's wool. Now place the pod onto the pipe cleaner and sew it to the main stalk.

Cut the leaf out of green felt. Shave the hairs off the green pipe cleaner and glue it to the underside of the leaf, leaving approximately $5/8$ in (1.5 cm) sticking out. Attach this piece of wire to the stalk by winding florist's tape around them both.

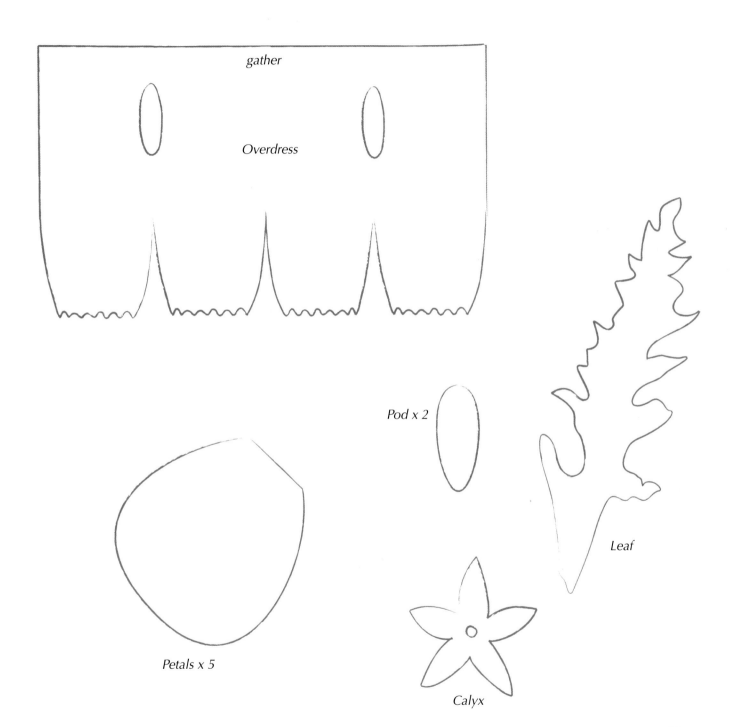

gather

Overdress

Pod x 2

Leaf

Petals x 5

Calyx

Bluebell child

Flower child

MATERIALS
For basic pattern, see *Flower child with legs*
Light blue cotton fabric for the dress
Light blue felt for the overdress
Yellow magic wool for the hair

Make the body according to the instructions for *Flower girl with legs*. Head circumference is 2 3/4 in (7 cm). Before covering the head with cotton knit, take a length of craft wire, bend it in half, twist it together lightly and place it around the neck from the back to the front. Pull tight, twist together twice and bring the ends to the back again. Twist at the back of the head a final time and cut the ends off. This allows you to easily bend back the head to make the child look upwards.

Cut the dress out of light blue cotton fabric, sew it together and put it on your flower child. Hem the neck opening and the sleeves with a gathering thread.

Cut the overdress out of felt and put it on. Run a gathering thread around the dress below the arms, pull tight and sew the ends in well.

Bluebell with butterfly

MATERIALS
Light blue felt for the flowers
Green felt for leaves and calyxes
Craft wire
Florist's tape
Strong thread
Yellow felt for the butterfly
Yellow buttonhole silk for the feelers

Cut 3 sets of the flower out of light blue felt. Glue each flower together as shown in the diagram and let them dry well. Leave a small opening at the bottom of each flower.

Wind florist's tape around a double, 4 3/4 in (12 cm) long, piece of craft wire (bend a 9 1/2 in (24 cm) long piece of wire in half and twist together lightly).

To make the shorter stalks, wind florist's tape around a 3 in (8 cm) long piece of craft wire (bend it in half first) and then attach it to the main stalk by winding florist's tape around them both. Make the third stalk in the same way.

Push the calyxes over the stalks. Add the flowers and glue the open bases to the stalks. Glue pieces of strong thread, approximately 5/8 in (1.5 cm) long, into the flowers for the pistils. Push the calyxes up to the flowers and glue it tight.

Attach the leaves to the meeting points of the stalks.

Cut the butterfly out of yellow felt. Glue two threads of buttonhole silk along the centre line, leaving a short bit sticking out at one side to make the feelers.

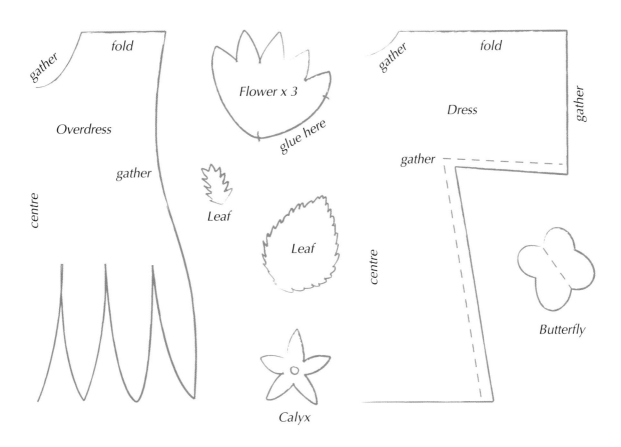

Snap Dragon child

Flower child

MATERIALS
For basic pattern, see *Flower girl with long skirt*
Pink felt (plant dyed) for the dress
Dark red felt for the jacket
3 small purple transparent glass beads
Curly baby sheep's wool for the hair

Make the body according to the instructions for *Flower child with long skirt*. Head circumference is 3 in (8 cm). Use the pattern provided for the sleeve edging.

Cut the jacket out of dark red felt and put it on the flower child. Sew three glass beads to the right side.

Flower

MATERIALS
Craft wire
White felt
3 oblong beads
Dark red felt for the calyxes and leaves
Pink silk $2/8$ x $3/8$ in (0.6 x 0.9 cm) for the flowers
White sewing silk

Florist's tape
Transparent craft glue

Cut two sets of the flower pattern out of pink silk.

Take a 9 1/2 (24 cm) long piece of wire for the stalk, bend it in half and twist together lightly. Wind a thin strip of white felt around the top end for 5/8 in (1.5 cm). Sew 6 loops of sewing silk to it for the filaments; cut them open once the flower is finished. Push the flower, with a small cross cut into the centre, almost up to the filaments from the bottom of the stalk and glue it tight.

Now thread an oblong bead to the stalk from below for the calyx, push it up to the white felt and glue tight. Glue dark red felt around it. Wind florist's tape around the rest of the stalk.

Cut three sepals out of dark red felt and glue them below the bead.

Make the second open flower in the same way, but make the stalk 2 in (5 cm) long (use a length of 4 in (10 cm) wire bent in half and twisted together lightly). Position it one third down the main stalk and wind florist's tape around both of the stalks. Glue two dark red felt leaves to the meeting points.

For the closed flower, take a 1 1/4 in (3 cm) long piece of craft wire (2 1/2 in (6 cm) bent in half and twisted together lightly). Place a bead over the top end of the wire and glue half of it tight, leaving the other half to glue the flower into. Roll up a thin piece of silk for the closed flower and glue it into the bead, leaving 3/16 in (0.5 cm) sticking out. Now glue the dark red felt around the bead for the calyx, wind florist's tape around the stalk and glue the sepals to the calyx base.

Position the stalk with the closed flower between the other stalks and wind florist's tape around them all.

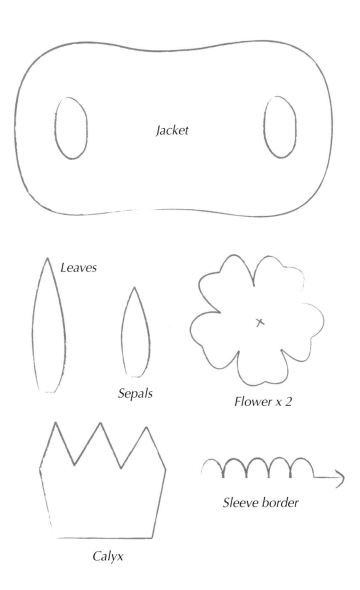

Jacket

Leaves

Sepals

Flower x 2

Calyx

Sleeve border

Plantain child

Flower child

MATERIALS

For basic pattern, see *Flower boy with legs*
Brown chenille fabric for the suit
Brown felt for the slippers
Alder cones
Yellow buttonhole thread
Tulle for the bee wings

Make the body according to the instructions for the *Flower boy with legs*. The head circumference is 2 3/4 in (7 cm).

Cut two sets of the suit pattern out of brown chenille fabric. Check the nap direction and cut the fabric with the nap, not against it. Sew the pieces together. Put the suit on the doll and run a gathering thread around the neck.

Make small brown slippers out of brown felt and glue them to the feet.

Make the bee held in one hand of the flower boy by winding yellow buttonhole thread loosely around a small alder cone. Cut the wings out of tulle and glue them to the top of the bee.

Flower

MATERIALS

Craft wire
White sewing thread
Thick, hairy brown or brown/yellow yarn for the spike
Green felt for the leaf
Florist's tape
Transparent craft glue

Use the following knotting technique to make the spike of the plantain flower: Cut two approx-imately 20 in (50 cm) lengths of brown yarn. Place one of the lengths between your forefinger and middle finger (thread 2) and middle finger and ring finger (thread 3), with both ends hanging down over the back of your hand. Place the other thread between your ring finger and little finger of the same hand with one end hanging over the back of your hand (thread 4) and the other end hanging over your palm (thread 1).

Take thread 1 and loop it around your thumb from front to back. Now guide thread 1 under thread 2 and thread 3 and over thread 4. Take thread 4 and place it over thread 3. Take thread 3 and place it over thread 2. Take thread 2 and draw it down through the thumb loop from above.

Carefully take the threads off your fingers and pull them into a flat knot.

Place this knot into your left palm. Put the rightmost thread between your little and ring fin-ger (thread 4), the next thread between ring and middle finger (thread three), the second thread between middle and forefinger (thread 2) and leave the left thread hanging down over your palm (thread 1).

Take thread 1, loop it around your thumb towards the back and place it over thread 2, then place thread 2 over thread 3, and thread 3 over thread 4 in the same way. Take thread 4, bring it round the front and draw it down through the loop around your thumb from the top. Carefully remove all the threads from your fingers and pull the knot tight above the previous knot.

To make the spike, repeat the above steps. Pull the first 3–5 knots very tightly, depending on the type of yarn. Make the further knots increasingly looser so that the spike becomes thicker towards the base. Continue making knots until the spike is approximately 1 ¼ in (3 cm) long. Leave the ends of yarn hanging loose.

To make the stalk, bend a piece of craft wire 10 ¼ in (26 cm long) in half and twist the ends together. Flatten the loop at the top with a pair of pliers. Then wind florist's tape around the stalk.

Put craft glue over the top end of the stalk and push it into the knotted plantain spike. Press the wool around the stalk. Apply glue to the base of the spike and cut the yarn ends off. The glue will stop the knot from unravelling.

To make the stamens, thread white sewing thread through a needle and push it back and forth through the spike just below the middle, leaving a small loop each time. Once finished, cut the loops apart.

Cut 2 sets of the leaf pattern out of green felt. Place a length of craft wire between the leaves and glue both leaves together. Once the leaf is dry, glue it to the base of the stalk and if necessary sew tight with a few stitches. To finish, twist the leaf lightly.

You can also make lamb's tail using this knotting technique.

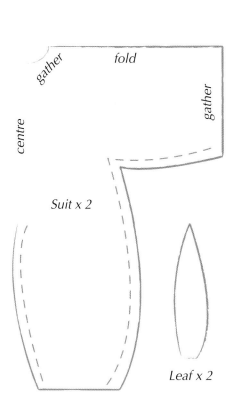

Edelweiss child

Flower child

MATERIALS

For basic pattern, see *Flower girl with legs*
White felt without synthetic fibres
1 black tea bag
Elastic lace or white felt for the underpants
Yellow magic wool for the hair
Transparent craft glue

Make the flower girl according to the instructions for *Flower girl with legs*. Dye the white felt (see flower instructions). Cut a second skirt border out of the dyed felt for the overskirt. Run a gathering thread around the top, pull tight around the waist and sew tight with a few stitches.

Flower

MATERIALS

White felt without synthetic fibres
1 black tea bag
8 pieces of craft wire, 4 in (10 cm) long

Florist's wire, 4 in (10 cm) long
Small bit of white magic wool
Small bit of light yellow magic wool
Light brown strip of felt, approximately 3/16 in
    (4 mm) long
Small piece of green felt
Transparent craft glue

Lightly dye a 3 x 3 in (8 x 8 cm) piece of white felt by briefly placing it in black tea (the felt will not dye if it is made with synthetic fibres). Rinse the felt well with clear water. Once dry, carefully roughen the felt with a pair of scissors to make it look 'hairy'. Now cut the flower out of the dyed felt.

To make the pistils, take 8 pieces of craft wire, 4 in (10 cm) long, and bend them in half. Unbend them again and wind a small bit of white and an even smaller bit of yellow magic wool around the bend. Then bend the wire in half again and twist the wool between your fingers until you've made a small, firm oval ball. Make 7 of these pistils and one slightly thicker one. Gather the pistils together, the thicker one in the centre.

Push the pistil stalks through the small cut cross in the flower and glue the flower to the pistils. Trim all the wire ends to the same length and glue the main stalk, 4 in (10 cm) florist's wire bent in half, between them. Once everything has dried well, cut a small strip of light brown felt, wind it below the flower around the stalk and glue.

Cut the leaves out of green felt and glue some white magic wool over the top to make the typically hairy surface. Glue a piece of wire to the leaves to make them sturdier and attach the leaves to the stalk.

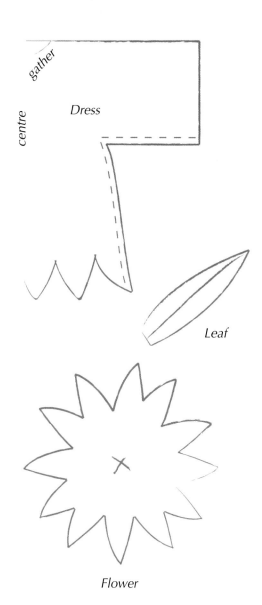

gather

centre

Dress

Leaf

Flower

Autumn

The little Root child continues along his journey. With great wonder he sees apple trees laden with red shiny fruit and smells the scent of ripe plums in the air. Squirrels gather nuts to hoard for the long, cold winter. The fat juicy blackberries entice him to taste them. But the sun is no longer strong enough for him to sit around and linger. The nights are fresh and in the early morning dewdrops dampen the meadows.

The moss king tells stories to the last remaining flowers and to animals who are still gathering their stores for the winter. These stories will accompany them during their long winter sleep, which they will soon embark on.

The first autumn storm takes the little Root child by surprise. He himself, not to mention his hat, is nearly blown away. In the sky he sees colourful kites being flown by children.

Once the sun sets, the little Root child gets quite cold and is glad that so many leaves have fallen to the ground. He uses them to make a comfortable, warm bed and lies down to rest. But in his dreams he continues along his journey through the seasons.

Blackberry child

MATERIALS
For basic pattern, see *Flower boy with legs*
Black and green felt
Green sewing thread
Black beads
Unspun white sheep's wool for the hair

Make the body according to the instructions for the *Flower boy with legs*. Head circumference is 2 3/4 in (7 cm).

Cut the trouser suit out of black felt and sew

together. Turn it right side out, put it on the flower boy and run a gathering thread around the neck.

Cut the leaf jacket out of green felt. Cut the front open and embroider the leaf veins as shown in the pattern. Put the jacket on the flower boy and sew it under the arms with two stitches. Sew the front of the jacket from the neck to the start of the stomach using mattress stitch, and attach 3 black beads to this seam.

Cut the hat out of black felt. Sew the back seam and completely cover the hat with black beads; if possible, do not leave any gaps.

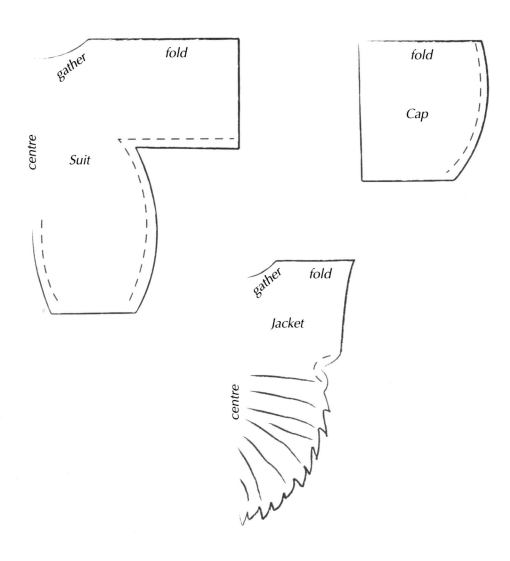

Acorn mother with child

Acorn mother

MATERIALS
For basic pattern, see *Flower girl with long skirt*
Brown felt for the dress
Green felt for the leaves
Brown magic wool for the hair

Make the acorn mother according to the instructions for *Flower girl with long skirt*. Head circumference is 2 3/4 in (7 cm). Make the dress out of brown felt using the pattern provided.

Cut three oak leaves, the apron bib and the apron strings, 3/16 x 4 in (0.5 x 10 cm), out of green felt. Embroider the leaf veins onto the leaves. Sew the leaves to the apron bib as shown (see diagram). Glue or sew the apron strings over them to cover the leaf stalks. Put the apron onto the acorn mother and sew the back seam. Cross the apron straps at the back and sew them underneath the apron strings. Leave the straps hanging out about 1 1/4 in (3 cm). See pattern overleaf.

Acorn child

MATERIALS
Light brown felt for the dress
White unspun sheep's wool for hair and stuffing
1 acorn cap

Make the head according to the instructions for the Snow gnome (page 84).

Cut two sets of the dress pattern out of light brown felt, sew the seams shut and turn right side out. Run a gathering thread around the neck edge. Stuff this small sack tightly with unspun sheep's wool and push the head of the acorn child into the top opening. Pull the gathering thread tight and sew the ends into the body.

Glue first the hair and then the acorn cap to the head. See pattern overleaf.

Honesty child

MATERIALS
For basic pattern, see *Flower girl with long skirt*
White felt for the dress
White silk for the skirt
White magic wool for the hair
Honesty seed pod stalk

Make the honesty child according to the instructions for the *Flower girl with long skirt*. The head

Pattern for Acorn mother with child

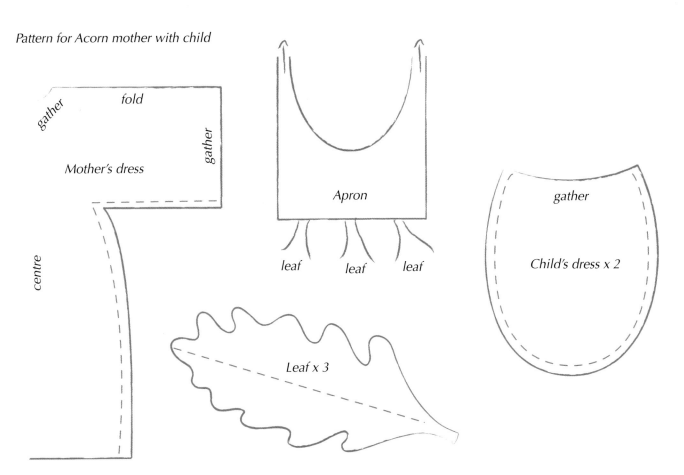

gather

fold

gather

Mother's dress

centre

Apron

leaf   leaf   leaf

Leaf x 3

gather

Child's dress x 2

Honesty Child

circumference is 3 in (8 cm). Make the dress out of white felt.

Cut out a 2 1/4 x 5 1/2 in (5.7 x 14 cm) piece of white silk for the skirt. Hem the edge and sew the back seam together. Turn the top edge down and run a gathering thread around it. Once you have put the skirt on the flower child, pull the gathering thread tight around the waist and sew in the ends.

Attach a real honesty seed pod stalk to one of the flower child's hands.

Rosehip boy

MATERIALS

For basic pattern, see *Flower boy with legs*
Red felt for the trousers, shirt and cape
Brown felt for the leaves
Black fake fur for the hair
Black sheep's wool for the shoes

Make the body according to the instructions for the *Flower boy with legs*. Head circumference is 3 in (8 cm), arm length 4 in (10 cm), leg length 2 3/8 in (6 cm). Make the hair using black fur.

Cut the trousers, shirt and cape out of red felt. Sew the shirt seams, run a gathering thread around the neck opening, turn right side out and put it on the boy. Now sew the trouser seams, turn right side out, run a gathering thread around the waist and put them on the boy. Run a gathering thread around the top of the cape. Pull the gathering thread until the cape reaches from shoulder to shoulder; sew it to the shoulders.

Cut the leaf collar out of brown felt, run a gathering thread around the top edge and sew it to the shoulders over the cape.

Wind black sheep's wool around the feet.

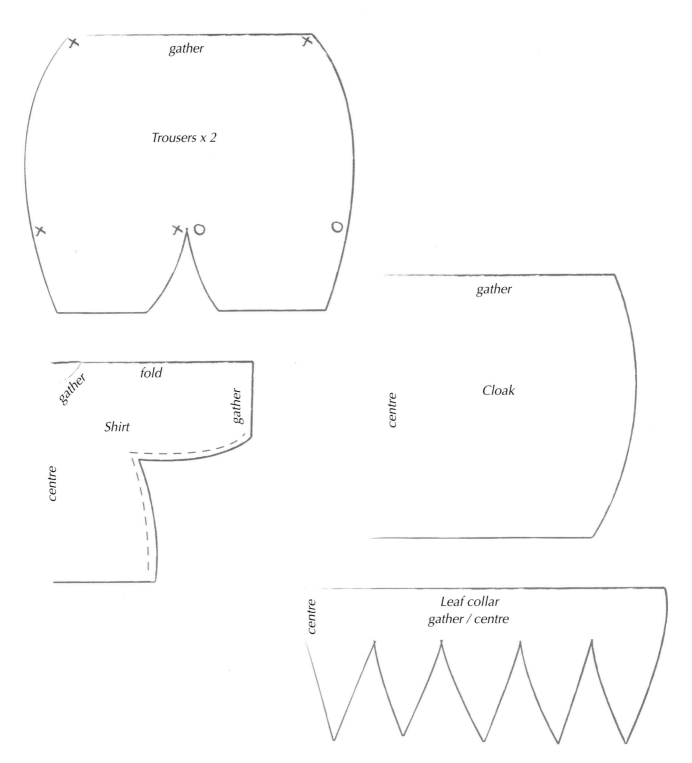

gather

Trousers x 2

gather

Cloak

centre

fold

gather

gather

Shirt

centre

centre

Leaf collar
gather / centre

Rosehip children

MATERIALS
Sheep's wool
Skin-coloured cotton knit
Black unspun sheep's wool
Brown felt for the collar
Red felt for body and cap

Make the head according to the instructions for the Snow gnomes (page 84), circumference approximately 1 1/2 in (4 cm). Do not tie off the eye and chin line.

Cut the body out of red felt and run a gathering thread around the edge. Pull it tight to make a sack with a small opening at the top. Stuff it well with sheep's wool. Push the head into the opening. Pull the gathering thread tight and sew in the ends well.

Cut the collar out of brown felt and sew it in place with a few stitches.

Cut two sets of the cap pattern out of red felt, sew the seam and turn right side out. Glue it to the head, positioning the seams to the left and right of the head.

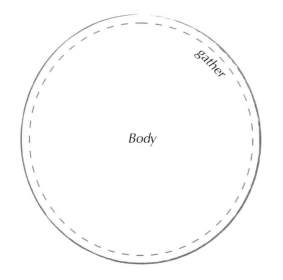

Body

gather

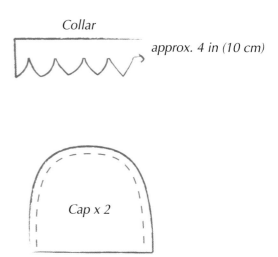

Collar

approx. 4 in (10 cm)

Cap x 2

Tree child

MATERIALS
Piece of round hollow bark
Material for a head (see *basic patterns*)

Make a head, circumference 2 in (5 cm), according to the instructions given in the basic patterns. Cut a small window into the piece of bark. Glue the head into the window.

Moss king

MATERIALS
Material for a head (see *basic patterns*)
Skin-coloured cotton knit for hands
Green felt for the dress
Dark brown chenille fabric for the cloak
Pipe cleaners, 8 in (20 cm) long
Green cardboard for the crown
Grey unspun sheep's wool for the hair

Make a head, circumference 4 3/4 in (12 cm). Before putting on the cotton knit, sew a small bead just below the eye line to make a knobbly nose.

Cut a green felt rectangle, 7 x 4 1/2 in (18 x 11 cm), for the dress. Sew the back seam and run a gathering thread around the neck opening. Push the head into this opening, pull the gathering thread tight and sew the ends of the thread in well.

Cut a rectangle, 3 3/8 x 6 in (8.5 x 15 cm) out of green felt for the sleeves. Sew together lengthwise and turn right side out. Push an 8 in (20 cm) long pipe cleaner through the sleeves and bend back the ends by 3/8 in (1 cm). Wind sheep's wool around the ends of the pipe cleaners for the hands. Cut two cotton-knit circles approximately 2 in (5 cm) circumference and pull over the hands. Smooth out the folds as well as possible and tie off the hands with a strong thread. Sew the arms to the centre of the back of the doll.

To make the cloak, cut a 7 x 10 in (18 x 25 cm) rectangle out of green chenille fabric. Run a gathering thread 3/4 in (2 cm) below the edge of the fabric along the shorter side and fasten it to the dress just before the shoulder blades. Cut small slits, unevenly spaced, into the top edge. This will make it unfurl slightly.

74

Sew hair and beard wool to the head. To make the eyebrows, take small pieces of sheep's wool, add some craft glue and twist between your fingers. Let them dry before glueing them to the face.

Cut the crown out of green cardboard, glue chenille fabric to it and cut the fabric into shape. Measure the head circumference and glue the crown together.

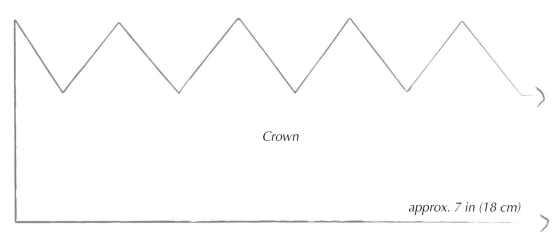

Crown

approx. 7 in (18 cm)

Moss boy

MATERIALS
For basic pattern, see *Flower boy with legs*
Green chenille fabric for the trousers and jacket
Green magic wool for the hair

Make the body according to the instructions for the *Flower boy with legs*, head circumference 2 3/4 in (7 cm).

Cut the trousers and jacket out of green chenille fabric. Sew the trouser leg seam, turn right side out and put the trousers on the boy. Run a gathering thread around the waist. Sew the jacket seams, turn right side out and put it on the boy. Sew the front shut using mattress stitch and run a gathering thread around the neck opening.

Make feet out of cotton knit using the same pattern as for the hands.

Sew on a beard and hair out of green magic wool.

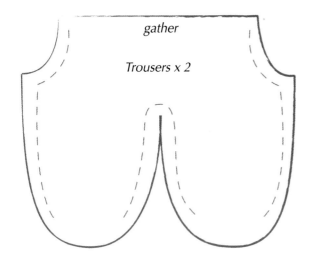

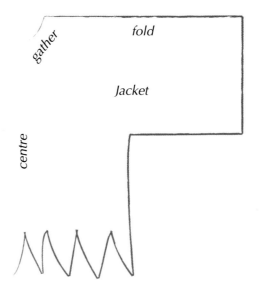

Maple boy

MATERIALS

For basic pattern, see *Flower boy with legs*
Green felt for the jacket
Rust red felt for the smock and trousers
Light brown fake fur for the hair
2 maple seeds

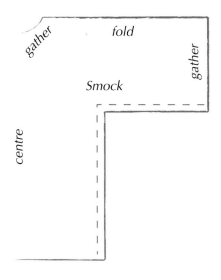

Make the body according to the instructions for the *Flower boy with legs*. The head circumference is 1 3/4 in (4.5 cm).

Cut the smock and trousers out of rust red felt, sew the seams and put them on the maple boy. Cut the jacket out of green felt and sew sleeves and part of the sides together with blanket stitch (see pattern).

Make the hair out of fake fur (see basic patterns, page 18).

Glue maple seeds to the shoulders.

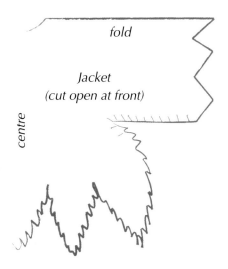

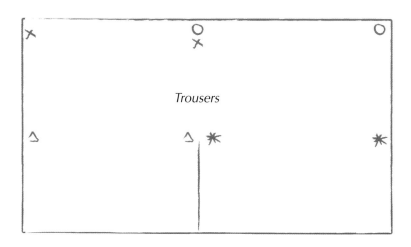

Bulb child

MATERIALS
Unspun sheep's wool
Thin cotton-knit tube
Skin-coloured cotton knit
Brown felt for the body, cape and hat
Green felt for the seedling
Transparent craft glue

Make a head, 1 3/4 in (4.5 cm) circumference, following the basic pattern on page 8. Use the thin cotton-knit tube. Trim the hanging out sheep's wool.

Cut two sets of the body semicircles out of brown felt. To make the body, sew part of the semicircle seam, leaving a hole large enough for stuffing. Run a gathering thread around the top and put the head in this opening. Pull the gathering thread tight and sew the ends in. Stuff the small sack lightly with sheep's wool and then sew the gap shut using mattress stitch.

For the cape, run a gathering thread along the straight edge and pull it until the cape reaches from shoulder to shoulder. Sew to the left and right of the shoulders.

Fasten a thin layer of sheep's wool to the head for hair.

Cut two sets of the hat pattern out of brown felt, sew it together (see diagram) and turn right side out.

Cut the seedling leaf out of green felt and glue it between the brown seed leaves on the cap. Let it all dry well and then twist the leaves lightly between your fingers.

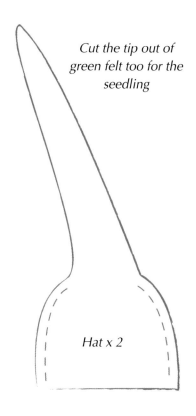

Cut the tip out of green felt too for the seedling

Hat x 2

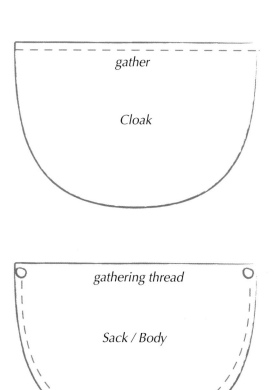

gather

Cloak

gathering thread

Sack / Body

Winter

One morning the Root child wakes up and sniffs the air. Something smells different. He looks around him and everything he sees is white. Little flakes are dancing merrily through the air and falling to the ground, making the white layer of snow ever thicker. All around is peaceful and quiet.

The ice princess has transformed the world into a glittering magical landscape. Ice-crystal children, ice gnomes and icicle boys play happily in the cold. Apart from the Christmas rose, which proclaims the coming Christmas festival, all the flowers have retreated deep into the earth. The animals, too, are sleeping in their dens waiting to be awakened by the warm spring sunshine. They are dreaming about spring with its many colourful flowers, a summer full of warmth and delicious smells and an autumn with ripe fruits and rich colours. They dream about the sun warming them up, the pretty clouds in the sky and of course the moon and stars at night.

The little Root child rubs his nose, looks for a warm, cosy cave and thinks about which season he has enjoyed the most. Which do you think has been the best?

Ice princess

MATERIALS
For basic pattern, see dress and body of *Flower girl with long skirt*
White felt for the dress
Fine white lace for the overdress and cape
Silver foil
Glass ball or round bead

Unspun silk for the hair
Skin-coloured sewing thread
Transparent craft glue

Make a flower girl according to the instructions for the *Flower girl with long skirt*. Head circumference is 3 in (8 cm). Make the dress out of white felt.

Cut out a rectangular piece of lace, 3 3/4 x 10 in (9.5 x 25 cm). Keep the edging at the bottom to stop the lace fraying. Sew the two shorter sides together. Arrange the lace so that the seam is at the back, and then cut two small arm slits into the lace right and left at arm height. Run a gathering thread around the top edge and put the overdress on the doll. Pull the gathering thread tight and sew in the ends.

For the cape, you will need a rectangular piece of lace 4 3/4 x 5 1/2 in (12 x 14 cm). Fold back the top edge approximately 3/8 in (1 cm) and run a gathering thread around it — the fabric will be

Ice princess

Ice-crystal children

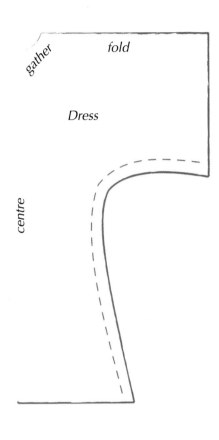

gather *fold*

Dress

centre

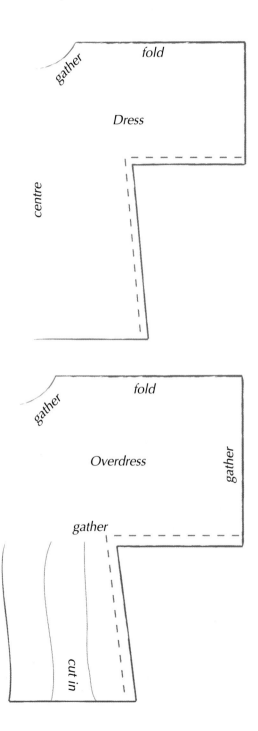

gather *fold*

Dress

centre

gather *fold*

Overdress

gather

gather

cut in

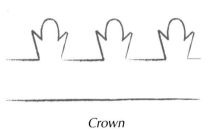

Crown

double here. Pull the gathering thread tight until the cape fits the shoulders, sew it tight to the right and left of the shoulders. The cape should be slightly longer than the ice princess.

Use unspun silk for the hair. Sew it to the head with small stitches.

Sew the hands together using skin-coloured thread. Glue or sew the glass ball on to the hands.

Cut the crown out of silver foil. Stamp the dots into the foil using a blunt needle. Glue the crown together at the back and put it on the princess.

Ice-crystal children

MATERIALS
For basic pattern, see *Flower girl with long skirt*
Fine white lace for the overdress
Pipe cleaners
Unspun silk for the hair
Stuffing wool

Make a head 2 1/2 in (6 cm) circumference according to the instructions given in the basic pattern.

Cut the dress out of white felt and sew it together, turn right side out. Push the head through the neck opening, run a gathering thread around the neck opening and pull tight. Push a pipe cleaner through the armholes, bend the ends back, and proceed as described in the basic pattern. Do not sew the hands, make as described for the Moss king (page 74). Lightly stuff the dress with stuffing wool. Run a gathering thread around the body below the arms and pull together slightly.

Sew the overdress out of white lace, turn right side out and put it on the doll. If necessary run a gathering thread below the arms too. Cut small slits into the overdress every 3/16 in (0.5 cm) from the bottom to the waist to make the crystal tips.

To make the ruff, cut a piece of lace approximately 3/8–5/8 in (1–1.5 cm) wide. The length depends on your preference. Run a gathering thread around the top edge and pull tight around the neck. Cut small slits into the ruff every 3/16 in (5 mm) and then taper the tips. For a picture of the Ice-crystal children, see the Ice princess (page 81).

Icicle boy

MATERIALS
For basic pattern, see *Flower boy with legs*
White velour fabric for the suit and shoes
White fake fur
White pipe cleaners
White candle

Make the body according to the instructions for the Flower boy with legs. Head circumference is 2 in (5 cm). Make the arms and legs to fit the garment pattern.

Cut the suit out of white velour fabric, sew together, turn right side out and put it on the doll. Run a gathering thread around the neck and sleeves and pull tight.

Cut the shoes out of velour fabric and run a gathering thread around the edge. Cut the leg pipe cleaners until they stick out approximately 3/4 in (2 cm) below the suit legs and bend the ends back. Bend the feet into position, put the shoes on and pull the gathering thread tight until there is a small hole at the front. Sew this hole shut with a few stitches.

For the icicles, cut the white pipe cleaner into three parts: 2 x 3 in (8 cm) and 1 x 1 1/2 in (4 cm). Bend the two longer pieces in half and place them over the shoulders of the icicle boy. Slowly drip candle wax over the pipe cleaners. Let the wax dry before dripping a second layer. Drip wax over the shorter pipe cleaner too and glue it the front of the chest. If necessary you can also glue the two longer icicles to the shoulders.

Snow gnomes

MATERIALS
White plush fabric for the coat
Unspun sheep's wool
Skin-coloured cotton knit

Cut the coat out of plush fabric. Sew the hood using small blanket stitches and run a gathering thread around the coat below the hood (see pattern).

Make a knot in the centre of a small piece of unspun sheep's wool. Take the upper strand of wool hanging out of the knot and arrange the wool over and around the knot. Tie the head off just below the knot with a few strands of sheep's wool or sewing thread. Place some cotton knit over the front of the head. Pull it to the back and bind it all off at the neck. Sew the cotton knit together at the top and back with a few small stitches.

Sew the sheep's wool beard to the hood with a few stitches. Divide the beard into three parts and twist each one between your fingers to make them look like small icicles. Put a drop of craft glue onto the tip of the hood and twist between your fingers too.

Push the head into the hood, pull the gathering thread tight and sew in the ends. Sew the coat shut using small blanket stitches. Cut back any surplus sheep's wool and run a gathering thread around the neck.

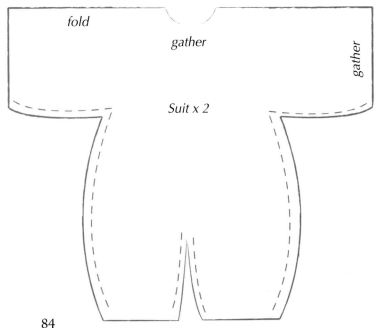

fold

gather

gather

Suit x 2

Mistletoe child

Flower child

Materials

For basic pattern, see dress and body of *Flower girl with long skirt*
Light beige velour for the coat and hat
White felt for the underskirt

Make the flower girl according to the instructions for the *Flower girl with long skirt*. Head circumference is 3 in (8 cm). Use the pattern given for the dress.

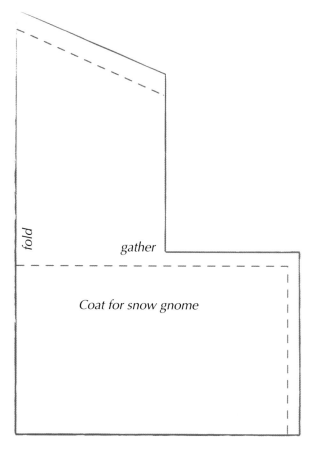

fold

gather

Coat for snow gnome

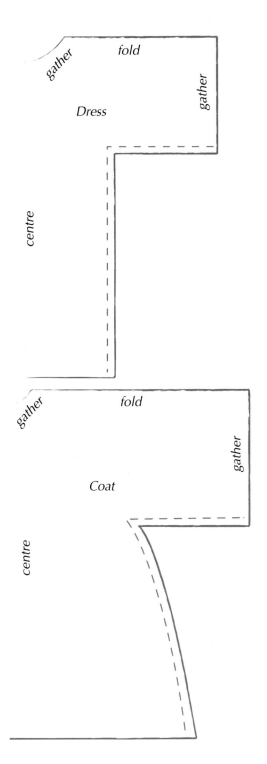

gather   fold

Dress

gather

centre

gather   fold

Coat

gather

centre

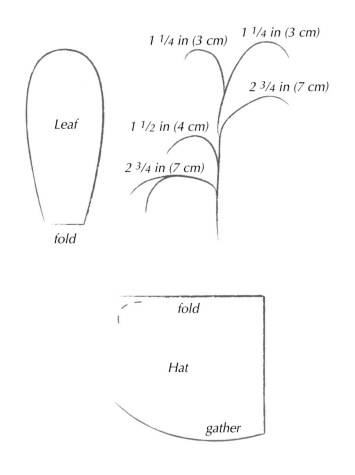

Leaf

fold

1 1/4 in (3 cm)   1 1/4 in (3 cm)

2 3/4 in (7 cm)

1 1/2 in (4 cm)

2 3/4 in (7 cm)

fold

Hat

gather

Cut the underskirt out of white felt and sew together. Now cut the coat and hat out of velour. Check the nap direction and cut the fabric with the nap, not against it. Sew the coat together and put it on the doll. Run a gathering thread around the neck and pull tight.

Sew the back seam of the hat, run a gathering thread around the lower edge and pull tight, make sure the face is still visible. Sew in the ends of the gathering thread. Sew the hat to the coat with mattress stitch.

Mistletoe twig

MATERIALS
Pipe cleaners
Florist's tape
Green felt for the leaves
Craft wire
Mother-of-pearl beads
A small piece of yellow felt
Transparent craft glue

To make the branched stalk, take a pipe cleaner and attach 4–5 further pipe cleaners to it by winding florist's tape around them all. Scrape the lint of the yellow felt with a pair of scissors, twist it into small balls and glue them to the top ends of the twigs.

Wind pieces of double craft wire so tightly around the stalk that they are hardly visible — wind them around the places where you later want to put the mistletoe berries. Glue the beads to the ends of the wire, leaving a small gap between berries and stalk.

Cut the leaves out of green felt (double the felt and cut the leaves with the stem towards the fold). Cut a small cross into the leaf fold and push the leaf over the stalk. Fold the leaves and glue them to the stalk, pressing them down well.

Christmas rose child

Flower child

MATERIALS
For basic pattern, see dress and body of the
   Flower girl with long skirt
White felt for the dress
White silk for the overdress
Unspun silk for the hair

Make the flower girl according to the instructions for the *Flower girl with long skirt.* Head circumference is 3 in (8 cm). Make the dress out of white felt.

Cut the overdress out of white silk and hem the bottom edge. Sew the back seam and put the dress on the doll. Fold the silk back at the sleeves. Run a gathering thread around the body below the arms and pull it tight. Fold the neck edge inwards and run a gathering thread around the neck opening.

Rose flower

MATERIALS
Green felt for the leaf and calyx
White felt for the flower
Craft wire, 4 3/4 in (12 cm) long
Pipe cleaner
Florist's tape or green felt
Yellow embroidery silk
Yellow fabric paint
Strong white thread for tying off
Transparent craft glue

Shave the pipe cleaner hair short and wind florist's tape or green felt around it.

Cut the flower out of white felt and glue a green circle of felt, circumference approximately 3/4 in (2 cm), to the centre as a receptacle. Embroider small embroidery silk loops over this circle for the stamens. To do this, sew the thread in at the back, and then bring the thread back to the front. Push the needle through to the back again, leaving a small loop at the front. Sew approximately 15–20 stamens, evenly spread out over the receptacle. In between, sew 15–20 slightly larger loops using tying off thread. Cut all the loops open. Dye the tips about 2/16 in (3 mm) using yellow fabric paint. Let the colour dry well.

Sew the petals together at the base as shown in the diagram. Sew the stalk firmly to the flower. Cut out the calyx. Cut a small cross into the centre and push it from below up the stalk to the flower. Glue it tight.

To finish, cut two sets of the leaf pattern out of green felt. Attach a piece of craft wire between the leaves and glue them together. Sew the leaf to the stalk.

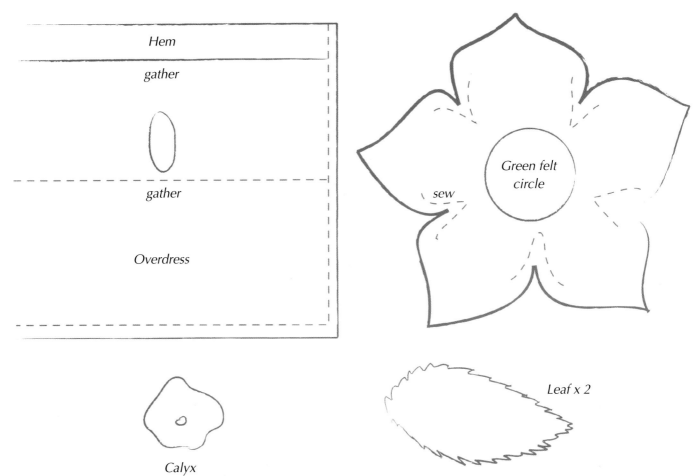

Hem

gather

gather

Overdress

sew

Green felt circle

Calyx

Leaf x 2